THE NATIVE AMERICAN COOKBOOK

Recipes From Native American Tribes

**Written And
Edited By
G.W. Mullins
With Original Art
By C.L. Hause**

LIGHT
OF THE
MOON
PUBLISHING

ISBN: 978-1-64007-710-2

Second Edition Printing

Light Of The Moon Publishing has allowed
this work to remain exactly as the author
intended, verbatim, without editorial input.

Printed in the United States of America

This book is dedicated to Vince Mullins, my Grandfather (Pawpaw). He was a tall red man with fire in his eyes... who I loved so much.

G.W. Mullins

This book is also dedicated to Chief Dan George, a true visionary.

**"May the stars carry your sadness away,
May the flowers fill your heart with beauty,
May hope forever wipe away your tears,
And, above all, may silence make you strong."
~ Chief Dan George**

Chief Dan George, (July 24, 1899 – September 23, 1981) was a chief of the Tsleil-Waututh Nation, a Coast Salish band located on Burrard Inlet in North Vancouver, British Columbia, Canada. He was also an author, poet, actor, and an Officer of the Order of Canada. At the age of 71, he was nominated for an Academy Award for Best Supporting Actor in Little Big Man.

Also Available From G.W. Mullins And C.L. Hause

Walking With Spirits Native American Myths, Legends, And Folklore
Volumes One Thru Six

The Native American Cookbook

Native American Cooking - An Indian Cookbook With Legends And Folklore

The Native American Story Book - Stories Of The American Indians For Children
Volumes One Thru Five

The Best Native American Stories For Children

Cherokee A Collection of American Indian Legends, Stories And Fables

Creation Myths - Tales Of The Native American Indians

Strange Tales Of The Native American Indians

Spirit Quest - Stories Of The Native American Indians

Animal Tales Of The Native American Indians

Medicine Man - Shamanism, Natural Healing, Remedies And Stories Of The Native
American Indians

Native American Legends: Stories Of The Hopi Indians
Volumes One and Two

Totem Animals Of The Native Americans

The Best Native American Myths, Legends And Folklore
Volumes One Thru Three

Ghosts, Spirits And The Afterlife In Native American Indian Mythology And
Folklore

The Native American Art Book – Art Inspired By Native American Myths And
Legends

Table of Contents

Introduction

Many people do not realize it, but
Native American foods are rich in
nutrition as well as heritage. Few
people know that over fifty percent of the foods we enjoy
today were used by the Indians centuries ago.

Many people's beliefs go back to textbooks and their
portrayal of the first Thanksgiving and Native American
Indians bringing corn and turkey as contributions. In truth
these foods were a small fraction of a true Native
American's diet.

Native Americans were not only experts at hunting wild
game, but they also were excellent farmers. They were
known to cultivate crops in high, arid desert regions that
required elaborate irrigation systems. Wild plants were also
used abundantly to supplement the diet. Nothing was
wasted, even the roots were often ground into powders to
be used breads and other foods.

Native American food consisted of three staples which
were corn, squash, and beans. Other foods that were widely
used include greens, Deer meat, berries, pumpkin, squash,
and wild rice.

Along with the staples and animal sources, herbs also
played a vital role in early Native American food. Many of
the earliest forms of medicine were derived from these food
sources as well. The Native Americans were masters at
making poultices, teas, and herbal remedies. They used
herbs and plants such as Peppermint, Spearmint, Clover,
Sage, and Rosehips to make teas and other foods.

Native Americans have always been well revered for being resourceful people, and when it comes to food, there is no difference. They were well versed at using the ingredients that were readily available to them and for making many different foods with them.

Native American delicacies have shaped American culture as a whole. Today's society owes much of what it has learned about food and the natural American resources to the early Native Americans. Included in this book are many recipes that cover a wide range of Native American cooking. Some recipes are tradition while others have been redeveloped over the years to include new ways of cooking and include new spices and ingredients. The recipes in this collection have been chosen in a way to stay true to the Native experience.

Enjoy these recipes and take a look back at a healthier nation. One which did not rely on processed foods. Experience true Native American flavor and creativity.

Drinks

Clover Tea

If Gathered: Gather when full grown, and dry at room temperature. When thoroughly dry grind into very fine particles, and seal in jars. This will help it to retain flavor. If you are unable to do this you can find Clover Tea at your local grocery store.

Use 1 tsp. to each cup of boiling water. Brew in a cup or a teapot (as you would other teas), and sweeten with honey.

Parsnip Wine

For the right flavor the parsnips have to be taken out of the ground in February. If you are unable to do this you can find parsnips at the grocery store.

1 quart grated parsnips
1 gallon boiling water
2 ½ lb. white sugar
¼ teacup liquid yeast

How to make liquid yeast: Add warm water to yeast to liquefy the yeast.

Put grated parsnips in a stoneware jar, and pour boiling water over them. Set jar on the back of the stove where it will keep hot, but will not boil. Leave it there 4 hours, then strain. Wash jar, then return the liquid to it. Add the sugar, and stir until dissolved. When it is lukewarm add the yeast. Let stand until seasoned (about 2 weeks or until fermentation stops).

Home Brew
5 gallon crock or wooden keg
1 quart of store-bought red top malt
4 gallons of water
5 lbs. of sugar
2 small cakes of yeast

Heat about a 1/3 of the water from above. In the crock stir the sugar and malt with the heated water until it has dissolved. Cool it down with the cooler water to a milk warm temperature. Add the 2 cakes of yeast, and keep in a warm place. It foams and works about 3 days. Then it stops and the foam goes down and it's ready to bottle.

Odds And Ends

Pickled Walnuts

Use about 100 walnuts or butternuts. Prick each with a needle well through, hold with cloth to avoid staining hands. Soak in salt water (1 ½ pints salt to 1 gallon of water) for 2 to 3 days changing the salt water each day. Then let stand for 3 days; drain and expose to sun for 3 days. After this pack in jars and cover with a gallon of vinegar that has been boiled with 1 cup sugar, 3 dozen cloves, 1 ½ dozen pepper corns, and a dozen blades of mace. Pour over walnuts while scalding hot. In three days, draw off vinegar, boil it, and pour over walnuts while hot. After 3 days repeat the last step. They will be ready to eat in one month. They will keep for a year.

Pemmican
Ingredients
Dried berries, 1/4 as much as jerky (Blueberries are good)
beef jerkysuet (enough to hold ingredients together)

Preparation
Shred the jerky finely with a sharp knife. be careful, this
can be hard.

If the berries are big chop them up too.
Melt suet and combine all ingredient to make soft blob.
Pour into a leather bag and cut off chunks when you need
them. Or pour into a pan lined with tinfoil and when cool,
unmold and cut into bars.
Store in the fridge.

Spiced Winter Squash Butter
3 medium acorn or other winter squash (about 3 pounds)
1/2 cup thawed undiluted concentrated apple juice
3/4 cup packed brown sugar
1/4 teaspoon ground cinnamon
1/4 teaspoon ground nutmeg
1/4 teaspoon ground ginger
1/8 teaspoon ground cloves

Preheat oven to 400 degrees. Cut squash in half lengthwise;
discard seeds and stringy pulp. Place squash, cut sides
down, in a pan. Cover and bake at 400 degrees for 1 hour
or until tender. Cool. Scoop out pulp to equal 3 cups. Place

pulp in a blender or food processor; process until smooth. Combine pureed squash, apple juice, and the remaining ingredients in a large saucepan, bring to a boil. Reduce heat, and simmer, uncovered, 45 minutes or until thick, stirring frequently. Cool. Store in an airtight container in the refrigerator. Will keep up to about 2 months.

Ham Curing

This recipe is enough to cure 8 hams.
Rub each ham well with a mixture of 8 quarts of salt, 16 tbsp. of black pepper, and 16 tbsp. of white sugar. Put some mixture into the shank bone. Wrap in brown paper and place in cloth bag. Hang with shank facing down.

Sweet Pickle Sticks

3 ¾ cups vinegar
3 tablespoons salt
4 ½ teaspoons turmeric
3 cups sugar
4 ½ teaspoons celery seed
¾ teaspoon mustard seed

Use fresh, firm, medium cucumbers. Wash and cut into quarters. Pour boiling water over them and let stand overnight. Next morning, pack solidly into clean jars. Make pickling solution, boil 5 minutes, and pour hot solution over cucumbers. Put on lids and seal. Fills 6 pint jars.

Green Tomato Pickles

Chop a half peck of tomatoes, 3 onions, a gill of horse-radish, 3green peppers; put in a sieve and drain dry. Salt in layers and let stand overnight. Drain them. Scald vinegar and pour over it; let stand two to three days then drain again. Mix quart of vinegar, one tablespoon of black pepper, the same of allspice, 3 ounces of ground cloves, three ounces of mustard, and a gill of mustard seed. Bring to a boil, and pour over the pickles and let stand.

Hominy Grits
1 cup hominy grits
1 teaspoon salt
5 cups boiling water

Cook slowly, 25 to 30 minutes, stirring frequently. Serve with gravy or with butter or with cream and sugar. Chill the leftovers; slice and fry in butter until golden brown.

Vegetables

Pickled Beans
Mix 2/3 cup of lemon juice, ½ cup oil, 2 teaspoon salt and pepper, 1 teaspoon dry mustard, ½ cup pearl onions. Add to 1lb. green beans (cooked briefly) in a crock. Let stand 4 days.

Sautéed Native Squash & Potatoes
1 lb summer squash
11/4 teaspoon sea salt; more to taste
1/4 cup extra-virgin olive oil
11/2 cups potato, peeled and diced
freshly ground black pepper
1/4 cup poblano pepper, finely diced
2 cloves garlic, minced
1/2 teaspoon chili powder
3 tablespoons chopped fresh cilantro

Wash the squash well to remove any grit and dry them with paper towels. Cube the squash Sprinkle with 1/2 tsp. sea salt and set aside for 10 minutes. Heat a large skillet (preferably 12 inches wide and cast iron) over medium-high heat for 1 minute. Pour in 2 Tbs. of the oil, add the squash, and sauté, stirring occasionally, until the squash browns and softens enough that you can cut through it with the side of a fork, about 4 minutes. Transfer to a large plate. Carefully dry the hot skillet with a paper towel. Add the remaining 2 Tbs. olive oil and the potato; season with 3/4 teaspoon salt and a few generous grinds of black pepper. Sauté, stirring occasionally, until the potatoes brown and cook through, about 7 minutes. Add the poblano pepper, garlic, and chili powder and sauté for 1 minute. Stir in the squash and cilantro and taste for salt and pepper. Serve immediately.

Cherokee Succotash
2 lb fresh or dry lima beans small ones are best
3 cups fresh corn cut from cob
4 pieces wild onions or pearl onions
2 tablespoons bacon fat; melted

Soak beans, if using dry ones, for 3-4 hours. Bring the water to a boil then add the beans. Cook at a moderate boil for 10 minutes then add the corn, ham hocks, salt & pepper, and onions. Reduce heat and cook for 1 hour on a low heat.

Cherokee Fried Hominy
Several Strips of Bacon
One or two Cans of White Hominy
Onion if desired
Black Pepper to taste
Preparation:
Fry bacon crisp. Remove from pan.
Drain most of grease. Drain water off hominy. Fry hominy in bacon grease.
Crumble bacon & mix in hominy.

Creamy Cabbage
8 cups shredded cabbage
1 cup milk
1 teaspoon salt
1 teaspoon celery seed
2 eggs (beaten)
2 tablespoon melted butter
¼ teaspoon pepper

Cover the cabbage with cold water and let stand for about 1 hour. Drain and put in large sauce pan. Cover with boiling water. Simmer uncovered for 7 minutes. Do not overcook. Combine the remaining ingredients and fold in the cabbage. Turn into buttered baking dish and bake for 30 minutes at 375 degrees.

Leather Britches Beans
Wash and drain a batch of firm green beans. Remove ends and strings. Use a large darning needle with heavy white thread through the pod near the middle of each pushing the along the thread so that they are about 1/4" apart. Hang up the strings of beans in a warm, well-ventilated place to dry. They will shrivel and turn a greenish gray. To cook in the winter time, cover with water, and parboil slowly for half an hour. Drain again. Cook slowly with ham hock or salt pork until tender. Serve with cornbread.

Dandelion Greens

The greens can be used until they bloom. Pick over carefully, and wash several times, changing water each time. Put them in boil water with a piece of salt pork, and boil for 1 hour. Drain well. Then put them in another batch of salted boiling water for 2 hours. When well done and tender, turn into colander and drain.

Squash and Corn with Tomatoes

1 1/2 tablespoons unsalted butter
3/4 pound zucchini cut into 1/2 inch slices
1 1/4 pounds summer squash cut into 1/2 inch slices
3/4 pound corn kernels (thawed if frozen)
1 1/4 pounds tomatoes, seeded and chopped
3 ounces canned green chilies, drained and thinly sliced
1 1/2 tablespoons minced cilantro or parsley

Melt butter in a heavy nonstick skillet over medium heat. Sauté zucchini, summer squash and corn 2 minutes. Add tomatoes, chilies and pepper to taste. Cover skillet and simmer 5-6 minutes or until zucchini is tender. Remove from heat. Stir in cilantro and serve.

Succotash

1 lb bag of (large) Lima beans,
1 16 oz can of Cream Corn
1 (small piece) Salt Pork (optional)
1/2 (small) Onion (cut fine)
2 tablespoons Butter

1/2 cup Sugar
Salt & Pepper (season to taste)
Preparation:
Wash lima beans and place in a large (5qrt) pot.
Add water(4 quarts), salt pork, butter, sugar, salt & pepper.
Bring to a boil.
Cook till beans are tender.
Add cream corn and cook additional 5 minutes.
Remove from heat and enjoy.

Batter-Fried Squash Blossoms
Ingredients for 8 servings
squash blossoms, picked as they are just about to open
(2-3 dozen)
1 cup milk
1/2 cup cooking oil
1 tablespoon flour
1/8 teaspoon fresh ground pepper
1 teaspoon salt

paprika (garnish)

1 In a shaker jar, combine milk, flour, salt and pepper. Place squash blossoms in large pan and gently pour the milk-flour mixture over them. Heat the oil in a large skillet until a drop of water will sizzle. Fry the batter-coated blossoms in the hot oil until golden brown, drain on paper toweling and sprinkle with paprika. Serve hot.

Acorn Squash With Raspberry Stuffing
1 piece large acorn squash
2 teaspoons extra-virgin olive oil
1/4 teaspoon pumpkin pie spice
1 cup brown ready rice
1/4 cup frozen raspberries
1 pc scallion, finely chopped
1 tablespoon frozen orange juice concentrate
1/4 cup chopped walnuts
1/4 cup light raspberry and walnut vinaigrette

Preheat oven to 400 degrees F. Cut squash in half and scoop out seeds. Use a pastry brush to brush squash with olive oil and sprinkle with pumpkin pie spice; set aside. In a large mixing bowl, stir to combine remaining ingredients. Fill centers of squash with stuffing mixture. Place in a baking dish and cover with foil. Bake in preheated oven for 45 minutes.

Remove foil and continue baking another 15 to 20 minutes or until squash is fork tender. Cut each half acorn squash into half and serve hot.

Alabama Corn Boil
8-12 ears corn un-shucked (trim silky end)
8-10 pieces onions (peeled)
8-12 pieces carrots (peeled)
8-10 pieces bell peppers (halved and seeded)
8-10 pieces potatoes (whole washed)
3 lbs. polish sausage cut into 4' pieces
3 lbs. Italian sausage cut into 4' pieces
1-2 lbs. fresh green beans (whole, washed)
water as needed
melted butter as needed

Stand the ears of corn on the stalk end around the perimeter of a very large pot. Place all of the other ingredients in the middle. You can actually add ingredients until the pot is full.

Add about one inch of water to the pot. Cover, set stove to low setting, and let cook/steam very slowly for four to five hours. No need to disturb during cooking.
Serve with melted butter (add garlic to butter if desired) for dipping.

Easy Corn Pudding
2 cups fresh corn
2 teaspoon sugar
1 ½ teaspoon salt
1/8 teaspoon pepper
3 eggs (slightly beaten)
2 tablespoons butter
2 cups milk

Combine the corn, sugar, salt, and pepper. Add the eggs and mix. Add the butter to the milk, then heat until butter is melted. Blend the milk with the corn and egg. Put into baking dish, and bake at 325 degrees for 1 hour or until knife comes out clean.

Winter Squash Soup

2 tablespoons lite margarine
1 cup finely chopped onion
2 teaspoons curry powder
3 pounds butternut squash, peeled and cut in to 1 inch pieces
2 cans (14 ounces each) defatted chicken broth
2 cups water
1 teaspoon peeled, grated fresh ginger
1/2 teaspoon ground pepper
1/2 cup plain nonfat yogurt

Melt margarine in a Dutch oven over medium heat. Cook onions 2 minutes, stir in curry powder and cook an additional minute. Stir in squash, broth, water, ginger and pepper. Increase heat to high and bring mixture to a boil; reduce heat and simmer 15-20 minutes, or until squash is tender. Puree this mixture in a blender in batches. Transfer each batch to a large bowl, then return to Dutch oven when last batch is pureed.

Simmer soup in the Dutch oven 5-10 minutes, or until heated through. Top each serving with 1 tablespoon yogurt, slightly mixed in.

Fried Sweet Potatoes
Peel and cut sweet potatoes. Put fat in skillet, keep turning potatoes. When almost done, add 3 to 4 teaspoons brown sugar and ¾ cup sweet milk. Place on low heat, let simmer until done. Best when served hot.

Three Sisters Stew
1 tablespoon olive or canola oil
1 large onion, sliced
1 clove garlic, crushed
1 jalapeno chili, finely chopped
4 cups yellow summer squash, sliced (about 1 pound)
4 cups zucchini, cut into 1 inch pieces (about 2 medium)
4 cups butternut squash, peeled and cubed (about 1 large)
3 cups green beans, cut into 1 inch pieces (about 1 pound)
1 cup frozen whole kernel corn
1 teaspoon dried thyme leaves
2 16-ounce cans kidney beans, un-drained

Heat oil in Dutch oven over medium heat. Cook onion, garlic and chili in oil about 2 minutes, stirring occasionally, until onion is tender. Stir in remaining ingredients. Cook over low heat 10-15 minutes, stirring frequently until squash is tender

Green Beans and Peppers
1 cup low-sodium chicken broth
4 cups fresh whole green beans or 16 oz. package frozen green beans
1 tablespoon margarine
1 medium red pepper cut into strips
¼ teaspoon garlic powder (optional)
salt and pepper to taste (optional)
2 tablespoons chopped parsley

If using fresh green beans, wash in cold water and snip off the ends. In a medium saucepan bring broth to a boil; add beans and cover. cook over medium heat for 8 12 minutes. If using frozen beans, time according to package directions. Melt margarine in a small skillet and add the pepper strips. Sprinkle in the garlic powder. Stir and cook until crisp-tender, about 6 minutes. Drain the green beans. In a serving bowl, add the cooked beans and pepper mixture; toss. Season with salt and pepper to taste. Sprinkle chopped parsley over the top.

Navy Beans
Wash the navy beans, and pick out the old ones. Put the good ones in a large pan with enough cold water to cover about 1". Boil at medium heat for one hour. (Check to

make sure the water continues to cover the beans, add if needed.) One-half hour after starting boiling, put 5 cups cold water in another pan and steak of fat. Turn on at medium heat and boil. After the beans have cooked the first hour, pour the remaining water off (should be very little) and add the meat and water mixture. Continue to boil at medium heat for almost another hour. In the last ten minutes, add salt. Turn the heat down and let simmer until serving, stirring occasionally.

Maple Mashed Sweet Potatoes
6 lb sweet potatoes
1 stick (1/2 cup) unsalted butter, melted
1/2 cup heavy cream, warmed
2 tablespoons pure maple syrup
1 teaspoon salt
1/2 teaspoon black pepper
Preheat oven to 400°F.

Prick each potato twice with a fork and bake in a foil-lined shallow baking pan in lower third of oven until very tender, about 1 hour. Remove and cool slightly. Halve potatoes lengthwise and scoop out warm flesh into a large bowl. Mash potatoes with a potato masher or, for a smoother purée, force through a potato ricer. Stir in butter, cream, syrup, salt, and pepper.

Hog Jowls and Turnip Greens (Southern Style)

Mustard, kale, and turnip greens are cooked same as spinach. Smoke hog jowl is then cooked with greens. Then season with red pepper and salt to taste. Cook until tender, drain and serve on platter with meat in center and poached eggs. It's usually served with cornbread.

Spiced Winter Squash Butter

3 medium acorn or other winter squash (about 3 pounds)
1/2 cup thawed undiluted concentrated apple juice
3/4 cup packed brown sugar
1/4 teaspoon ground cinnamon
1/4 teaspoon ground nutmeg
1/4 teaspoon ground ginger
1/8 teaspoon ground cloves

Preheat oven to 400 degrees. Cut squash in half lengthwise; discard seeds and stringy pulp. Place squash, cut sides down, in a pan. Cover and bake at 400 degrees for 1 hour or until tender. Cool. Scoop out pulp to equal 3 cups. Place pulp in a blender or food processor; process until smooth. Combine pureed squash, apple juice, and the remaining ingredients in a large saucepan, bring to a boil. Reduce heat, and simmer, uncovered, 45 minutes or until thick, stirring frequently. Cool. Store in an airtight container in the refrigerator. Will keep up to 2 months.

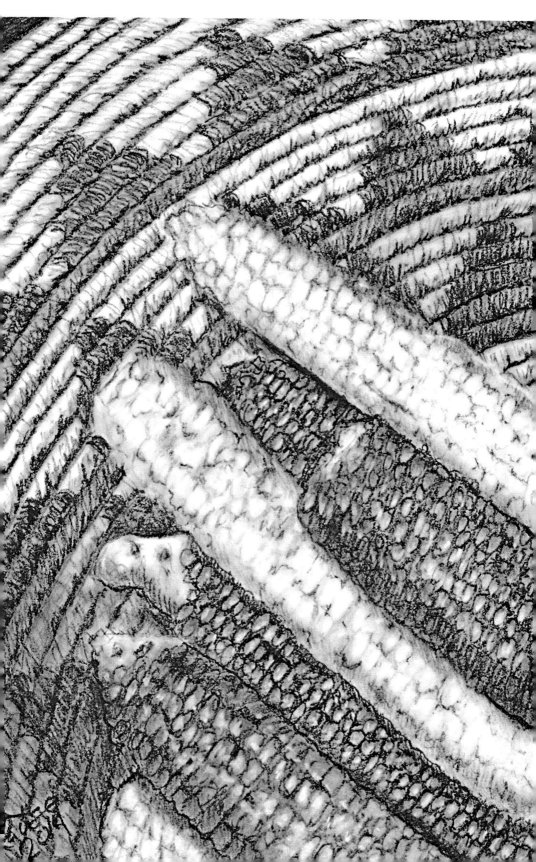

Soups and Stews

Apache Acorn Soup
3 lb Stew beef
2 qt Water
1 tsp Pepper
1 tsp Salt
1 cup Ground acorn meal

Cover beef with water and bring to boil in a heavy pot.
Simmer untildone; add salt and pepper as meat cooks
tender. Remove beef and chop on a flat stone until split in
shreds. The meat broth continues to cook vigorously while
meat and acorn flour (meal) are mixed together. Apaches
stress that their food is always well done; no instant
cooking. Broth, meat and meal simmer together until the
broth bubbles creamy white with yellow flecks, pleasantly
acorn scented and flavored.

Turtle Soup
Ingredients for 4 servings
1 pound frozen turtle or terrapin meat
2 scallions, washed and sliced (include tops)
2-1/2 quarts water
1 (4.5 gram) package instant beef broth
1/2 teaspoon salt

Place the turtle or terrapin meat in a large, heavy kettle.
Add the scallions and 1-1/2 quarts water. Simmer together

gently for 2 hours. Remove the meat from the broth, and dice. Return to the broth. Add 1 quart water, instant beef broth, and the salt, and simmer for 2 hours longer or until the meat is tender. Serve hot.

Chicken, Corn, And Potato Stew
1 (3 1/2- to 4-lb) chicken, cut into 8 serving pieces
1 3/4 teaspoons salt
1 1/2 teaspoons black pepper
3 tablespoons unsalted butter
1 large white onion, finely chopped
2 teaspoons dried oregano, crumbled
1 1/2 lb russet (baking) potatoes
6 cups chicken broth
1 cup water
2 lb potatoes, peeled, cut into 1/2-inch cubes, and covered with water in a bowl
3 ears corn, cut crosswise into 1-inch pieces

Accompaniments:
1/2 cup chopped fresh cilantro leaves
1 cup heavy cream
3 tablespoons drained capers
3 avocados, quartered, pitted, peeled, and cut into 1/2-inch cubes

Pat chicken dry and season with 3/4 teaspoon salt and 1/2 teaspoon pepper. Heat butter in a wide heavy 7- to 8-quart pot over moderately high heat until foam subsides, then brown chicken in 2 batches, skin side down first, turning occasionally, about 10 minutes. Transfer chicken as browned to a plate.

Add onion to pot along with oregano and remaining teaspoon each salt and pepper and sauté, stirring, until light golden, about 5 minutes. Peel and coarsely grate russet potatoes and add to pot with chicken, broth, and water. Simmer, covered, stirring occasionally, until chicken is cooked through, about 25 minutes. Transfer chicken with tongs to a cutting board to cool. Drain cubed yellow potatoes and add to pot.

Simmer, covered, stirring occasionally, until cubed potatoes are almost tender, about 10 minutes. Add corn and simmer, covered, until tender, 5 to 10 minutes more. While corn is cooking, remove skin and bones from chicken and coarsely shred meat. Add meat to pot and heat through.

Black Bean Soup
1 cup sliced leeks
1/3 cup oil
2 cloves garlic, crushed
2 lb canned black beans
1/2 cup water
1 1/8 tsp fresh ground pepper

Sauté the leeks in the oil in a large saucepan until golden. Add garlic and half the beans with their liquid. Mash the beans with a fork. Then add the rest of the beans with their liquid but do not mash. Stir in the water, salt and pepper, and simmer, covered, for 40 minutes, stirring occasionally. Serve hot.

Seminole Pumpkin Soup
2 cups chicken stock
1/2 green pepper, diced
1 large tomato
1 green onion
1 sprig parsley
1/4 teaspoon thyme
2 cups cubed cooked pumpkin
1 tablespoon flour
2 tablespoons butter
1 cup milk
1/2 teaspoon nutmeg
1 teaspoon sugar
1/2 teaspoon salt

Place 1 cup chicken stock, green pepper, tomato, onion, parsley and thyme in blender. Cover and blend medium speed, just until vegetables are coarsely chopped. Put into a saucepan and simmer for 5 minutes.

Return mixture to blender. Add pumpkin and flour. Cover and use on high speed until mixture is very smooth. Pour mixture into saucepan. Stir in remaining 1 cup chicken stock and all remaining ingredients. Heat to a boil, stirring frequently. Cook 3 minutes longer. Serve hot. Serves 4 to 6

Pinto Bean Casserole

1 1/2 cups freshly cooked pinto beans, drained
1/2 cup diced green pepper
2 scallions, minced
1 teaspoon olive oil
2/3 cup diced tomato
1 teaspoon chili powder
1/2 teaspoon dried oregano
1/2 teaspoon ground coriander
1/2 cup egg substitute
1/4 cup (1-2 ounces) reduced fat sharp cheddar cheese

In a large saucepan over medium heat, sauté green pepper and minced scallion in olive oil for 5 minutes, or until soft. Stir in the drained pinto beans, tomato, chili powder, oregano and coriander. cook, stirring constantly, for 2 minutes. Remove from heat and stir in the egg substitute.

Coat a 2 cup casserole with vegetable cooking spray. Add the bean mixture and spread evenly. Sprinkle with shredded cheese. Bake at 375(F for 20 minutes, or until the filling is set.

Winter Squash Soup

2 tablespoons lite margarine
1 cup finely chopped onion
2 teaspoons curry powder
3 pounds butternut squash, peeled and cut in to 1 inch pieces
2 cans (14 ounces each) defatted chicken broth
2 cups water
1 teaspoon peeled, grated fresh ginger

1/2 teaspoon ground pepper
1/2 cup plain nonfat yogurt

Melt margarine in a Dutch oven over medium heat. Cook onions 2 minutes, stir in curry powder and cook an additional minute. Stir in squash, broth, water, ginger and pepper. Increase heat to high and bring mixture to a boil; reduce heat and simmer 15-20 minutes, or until squash is tender. Puree this mixture in a blender in batches. Transfer each batch to a large bowl, then return to Dutch oven when last batch is pureed.

Simmer soup in the Dutch oven 5-10 minutes, or until heated through. Top each serving with 1 tablespoon yogurt, slightly mixed in.

Desserts

Baked Pumpkin
1 small pumpkin, peeled and cut into cubes
1 cup sugar
1 teaspoon salt
Cinnamon

Place pumpkin cubes in a baking dish and sprinkle with sugar and salt. Cover pan with foil and bake in 325-degree oven until soft. Sprinkle with cinnamon.

Indian Spice Cake
2 cups sugar
3/4 cups bacon grease
2 cups water or milk
1 cup raisins
1 tsp cloves
1 tsp nutmeg
1 tsp allspice
1/2 tsp salt
3 1/2 cups flour
1 tsp baking soda
2 tsp baking powder
1 cup pecans (or other preferred nuts); chopped

Put sugar and bacon grease into a cast iron pot and heat. Stir in water or milk, raisins, cloves, nutmeg, allspice and salt. Bring to a boil and cook at boiling for 5 minutes, stirring occasionally. Remove pot from stove and allow to cool.

Sift together flour, baking soda and baking powder. Add this to cooled mixture and beat thoroughly. Stir in nuts. Pour batter into buttered baking pan Bake at 350 degrees F. for 40 minutes.

May be eaten plain or sprinkled with powdered sugar.

Native American Cinnamon Wild Rice Pudding
3 pieces eggs, beaten
3/4 c. dried cherries or raisins
1/2 c. maple syrup
1/2 tsp. ground cinnamon
1/4 tsp. ground nutmeg
1 tsp. vanilla
2 c. cooked wild rice
2 c. half and half or light cream, warmed
1/4 tsp. ground cinnamon
2 tbsp. sugar

Butter a 1 1/2-quart casserole. Set aside. Combine eggs, dried cherries or raisins, maple syrup, 1/2 teaspoon cinnamon, nutmeg, vanilla, rice and half and half. Stir gently. Pour into casserole. Mix 1/4 teaspoon cinnamon and sugar. Sprinkle on pudding. Bake at 350° for 1 hour. Serve warm.

Apple Relish

Grind 2 hot peppers and 5 onions. Add 1 tablespoon salt, and one cup boiling water. Let it stand 15 minutes and drain. Then add 14 large red apples that have been chopped with skins left on (cores removed), 1 quart vinegar, 1 cup sugar, and a cloth bag with tablespoon of whole spice, a tablespoon of cloves, and a stick of cinnamon inside. Cook for 10 to 15 minutes. Remove cloth bag and put in sterilized jars and seal.

Pumpkin Pie

2 eggs (slightly beaten)
¾ cup sugar
1 tsp. cinnamon
½ tsp. ginger
¼ tsp. cloves
1 ¾ cups pumpkin
½ tsp. salt
1 2/3 cup light cream
Unbaked pie shell

Mix in order listed, and pour into unbaked pie shell. Bake at 425 degrees for 15 minutes, then at 350 degrees for about 45 minutes or until inserted knife comes out clean. Let it cool and serve with whipped cream if desired.

Corn, Zucchini, And Tomato Pie

This pie is made from the overflowing bounty of the backyard garden. Fresh corn and zucchini seasoned with dill bake underneath Parmesan-crusted tomatoes to make a scrumptious entrée that can be served warm or at room temperature.

3 cups fresh, or frozen and defrosted corn kernels
5 small zucchini, cut into matchstick pieces
2 teaspoons salt
1 teaspoon freshly ground black pepper
1 tablespoon fresh dill weed
2 tablespoons melted butter
3 to 4 vine-ripened tomatoes, cut into 1/2-inch slices
1/2 cup freshly grated Parmesan cheese
1/4 cup dry bread crumbs
2 tablespoons olive oil

Preheat the oven to 375°. In a 13 by 9-inch ovenproof baking dish, combine the corn, zucchini, 1 teaspoon of salt, 1/2 teaspoon of pepper, the dill, and the melted butter, tossing to coat the vegetables.

Cover the vegetables with the tomatoes. Sprinkle with the remaining salt and pepper.

In a small bowl, combine the cheese and the bread crumbs. Sprinkle the mixture over the tomatoes and drizzle with the olive oil. Bake the pie for 30 minutes, or until the cheese is bubbling. Remove it from the oven, and let it stand for 5 minutes before serving.

Rhubarb Pie

Unbaked pie shell
2 cups cooked and cooled rhubarb
2 egg yolks
1 tablespoon corn starch
½ cup milk
1 cup sugar

Mix ingredients and stir thoroughly. Put these into the unbaked shell, dot top with butter and bake until firm. Top with egg whites beaten stiff with ¼ cup sugar. Return to oven until it's a golden brown. Bake at 350 degrees.

Green Tomato Pie

3 cups of sliced green tomatoes
1 ½ cup sugar
¼ tsp. salt
5 tsp. grated lemon rind
¼ tsp. cinnamon
5 tbsp. butter
1 unbaked pie shell

Arrange the tomatoes in layers in the pie shell. Mix the other ingredients together in a bowl and sprinkle each layer of tomatoes with this mixture. When the bottom crust is filled, cover with a top crust, and bake at 350 degrees for 35 to 40 minutes.

Squash Pie
1 pint boiled dry squash
1 cup brown sugar
3 eggs
2 tsp. molasses
1 tsp. butter
1 tsp. ginger
1 tsp. cinnamon
½ tsp. salt
1 pint milk

Beat eggs and add remaining ingredients. Bake as a custard pie (in an unbaked pie shell) in a 350 degree oven.

Pumpkin Pie
9-inch unbaked pie shell
1/2 Cup packed dark brown sugar
1 teaspoon ground cinnamon
1 teaspoon ground ginger
1/4 teaspoon ground nutmeg
pinch of ground cloves
1 16-ounce can pumpkin puree
1 1/4 Cups evaporated skim milk
3 large egg whites

Preheat oven to 450 degrees Fahrenheit. In a large bowl, beat all filling ingredients until no lumps remain. Pour into pie shell and bake 10 minutes. Reduce heat to 325 degrees Fahrenheit and bake 50 minutes more, or until a knife inserted in the center comes out clean. To avoid over browning of fluted edge, cover edge with narrow strips of aluminum foil. Remove foil during the last 15 minutes of baking.

Sweet Potato Pudding
Boil and smash 6 medium sweet potatoes. Add 2 whole beaten eggs, ¼ lb. butter, ¾ cup brown sugar, ½ cup milk, 2/3 cup flour, ¼ cup orange juice, and 1 tsp. vanilla. Put in buttered-greased shallow baking dish. Place thin slices of orange on top, and then bake for 30 minutes at 350 degrees or until slightly brown at the edges.

Bannock Recipe (Cree Nation Recipe.)
2 cups flour
1 tsp baking powder
1 pinch of salt
1/3 cup raisins
1 cup water or milk
1 tbsp vegetable oil

Mix dry ingredients together in a large bowl. Make a well in the centre. Pour in water or milk & vegetable oil Mix together and form dough into a ball. Flatten the dough ball and poke holes in the dough. Place on a baking sheet and bake for 20–30 minutes a…Mix dry ingredients together in a large bowl. Make a well in the centre. Pour in water or milk & vegetable oil Mix together and form dough into a ball. Flatten the dough ball and poke holes in the dough. Place on a baking sheet and bake for 20–30 minutes at 375 degrees F. Less

Blackberry Pan Pie
1 stick margarine
½ cup sugar
Blackberries (about 1 cup)
1 cup flour
1 tsp. salt
3 tsp. baking powder
Melt the margarine and sugar in a pan. Add the blackberries. Mix the flour, milk, sugar, salt, and baking powder and mix and pour over the blackberries. Cook at 350 degrees until the batter is set.

Cranberry& Pumpkin Cake

1/2 cup chopped walnuts
3 tablespoons brown sugar
1 1/2 tablespoons toasted wheat germ
1/4 teaspoon pumpkin-pie spice
1 cup all-purpose flour
1/2 cup whole wheat flour
1/2 cup toasted wheat germ
2 teaspoons baking powder
1 teaspoon pumpkin-pie spice
3/4 teaspoon salt
1/4 teaspoon baking soda
1 cup plain fat-free yogurt
3/4 cup canned pumpkin
1/2 cup packed brown sugar
2 tablespoons vegetable oil
1 large egg
1/2 cup sweetened dried cranberries (example: Craisins)
1 teaspoon grated orange rind
cooking spray

Preheat oven to 350 degrees F. combine first 4 ingredients in a small bowl; stir and set aside. Combine flours and the next 5 ingredients in a medium bowl; make a well in center of mixture. Combine yogurt, pumpkin, 1/2 cup brown sugar, oil and egg; stir well with a whisk. Add to flour mixture, stirring just until moist. Fold in cranberries and orange rind. Spoon batter into a 13x9 inch cake pan coated with cooking spray. Sprinkle with walnut mixture. Bake at 350 degrees for 25 minutes. Cool on a wire rack.

Lakota Plum Cakes
1 cup dark raisins
1 cup boiling water
1 16-oz can purple plums, drained and pitted
1 cup toasted hazelnuts, chopped fine
1/2 cup melted butter
4 cups sifted all-purpose flour
3 teaspoons baking soda
1 1/2 tsp. salt; 1 1/2 tsp. allspice; 1 tsp. ground cloves
1 cup honey
1/2 cup maple syrup

Preheat oven to 350 degrees F. Place raisins in small glass bowl, cover with 1 cup boiling water; soak 30 minutes till plump. Lightly oil 24 or more muffin cups. Mash plums in a large mixing bowl, add remaining ingredients to plums and mix well. Add soaked raisins and their liquid. Blend together well. Fill each muffin cup 1/2 way full. Bake 30 minutes, or until a toothpick inserted in center comes out clean. Cool 10 minutes on wire rack, loosen sides, and turn out of muffin pan. Serve warm with honey or raspberry-plum butter.

Blue Corn Flapjacks
Two eggs
1 1/2 cups milk
1 tablespoon butter
3/4 cup all-purpose flour
3/4 cup blue roasted cornmeal
1 1/2 teaspoons baking soda
2 tablespoons sugar
1 teaspoon salt

Mix all ingredients in a blender. Let stand for 5 minutes. Do not re-mix or stir. Pour serving sized amounts from blender to lightly oiled grill.

Wait until bubbles form on top of flapjack then flip artfully with a great flourish and considerable bravado.

Remove from grill when second side is cooked. Serve topped with a pat of butter and syrup, marmalade, applesauce, or whatever.

Indian Cake
6 cups water
2 cups precooked yellow corn meal
1 cup sprouted wheat
4 cups precooked blue corn meal
1/2 cups raisins
1/2 cup brown sugar
Preparation:
Put 6 cups of water in pan and boil
Add 4 cups precooked blue corn meal
Add 2 cups precooked yellow corn meal
Add 1/2 cup raisins
Add 1 cup wheat, sprouted

Add 1/2 cup brown sugar
Blend well; dissolve all lumps. Pour into baking pan that is lined with foil.
Cover with foil. Bake at 250 degrees for 4 hours. (Cake needs to cook slowly.)

Onondaga Corn Sticks
1 cup cornmeal
1/2 Cup molasses
1/3 Cup flour
1/2 tsp salt
1 cup milk
1 egg
2 tablespoons lard - melted

Mix together the cornmeal, flour, salt. Add milk, egg and lard; beat until smooth.

Fill well-greased corn-stick pans almost to the top (or pour into a greased 8 in. pan). Bake in a preheated 425 F. oven for 12 to 15 minutes. Serve with butter, molasses or maple syrup.

Breads

Cherokee Huckleberry Bread
2 cups Self-rising flour
1 cup Milk
1 Egg
1 teaspoon Vanilla extract
1 cup Sugar
2 cups Berries (huckleberries or blueberries)
1 Stick of butter

Cream eggs, butter and sugar together. Add flour, milk, and vanilla. Sprinkle flour on berries to prevent them from going to the bottom. Add berries to mixture. Put in baking pan and bake in over at 350 degrees for approximately 40 minutes or until done.

Easy Molasses Bread
This bread is made by the quick one-rise method, which does not require any kneading. Adding blackstrap molasses appears to give it a slight sweetness and also makes it more nutritious. Suitable for freezing.

Makes 3 large (2-pound) loaves
butter or pure vegetable margarine
13 cups whole wheat flour
1 slightly heaping tablespoon salt
2 packets instant yeast
1 slightly heaping tablespoon molasses

Grease three large bread pans - or the equivalent, including cake pans, if you wish - generously with butter or margarine. Tip the flour and salt into a large bowl and add the yeast. Mix gently. Dissolve the molasses in a little tepid water taken from 6 1/4 cups. Add this to the flour, then mix in the rest of the water, going carefully at the end in case you don't need quite all of it. The finished mixture needs to be too wet to leave the sides of the bowl clean; it should feel 'slippery' but not completely sloppy. Half fill the pans with the mixture, cover them with plastic wrap or a damp dish towel, and leave to rise.

Meanwhile set the oven to 400°F. When the loaves have risen to within 1/2 inch of the tops of the pans, put them in the oven. Bake large loaves for 45 minutes, and small ones for about 35 minutes, or until they are brown and firm to the touch, and sound hollow when you slip them out of the pans and tap them on the base with your knuckles. If you wish, you can crisp the base and sides a bit more by putting the loaves back into the oven for a few minutes after you've taken them out of the pans. Cool the bread on a wire rack.

Apache Fry Bread Roll-Ups
4 pcs10-inch fry bread thin
2 tbsp. salad dressing or mayonnaise
1/2 c. chunky salsa
4 oz. sliced smoked turkey or roast beef
1/2 c. shredded cheese
1/2 c. thin strips red pepper
1/4 c. sliced green onions
2 tbsp. sliced pickled jalapeño

Spread salad dressing on fry bread; spread salsa over salad dressing. Top with meat, cheese and vegetables as desired. Roll up and serve or heat 1 minute in microwave on medium power. Wrap each fry bread in plastic wrap after rolling and then refrigerate. Cut into 1-inch slices for bite-sized snacks.

Frying Pan (Blue) Bread
11/2 cups flour
11/2 cups blue cornmeal (yellow may be substituted)
6 teaspoons baking powder
1 teaspoon salt
1/4 cup sugar
6 tablespoons grated cheese
1/4 cup chopped sweet green pepper
1/4 cup chopped onion
6 tablespoons shortening or cooking oil
4 teaspoons chili powder
1-1/2 cups milk
2 pieces eggs, slightly beaten

1 Sift dry ingredients, except Chile powder, in large bowl. Add green pepper, onion and cheese. In heavy skillet, melt shortening or heat cooking oil, mix in Chile powder. Cool, add milk and eggs. Stir mixture into dry ingredients until well blended. Return to skillet and bake in 400 oven for 35 minutes. Cut in wedges and serve hot.

Zucchini Bread
1 cup brown sugar
1/2 cup egg substitute

1/4 cup canola or safflower oil
1/4 cup natural, unsweetened applesauce
2 teaspoon vanilla extract
1 cup whole wheat flour
1 cup white, all-purpose flour
1/2 teaspoon salt
2 cups grated zucchini, drained
2 teaspoons baking soda
1 teaspoon baking powder
2 teaspoon ground cinnamon

Preheat oven to 350F. Combine brown sugar, egg substitute, oil, applesauce, vanilla, cinnamon and salt. Mix well. Stir in the grated zucchini, then the baking soda, baking powder, and flour. Optional raisins may be added at this stage. Blend gently. Pour into a nonstick baking pan sprayed lightly with vegetable cooking spray. Bake for 40-45 minutes or until a toothpick inserted near the center comes out clean. Cool for fifteen minutes in the pan then remove to cooling rack. Cool completely before slicing.

Wild Sage Bread
1 package dry yeast
1 cup cottage cheese
1 egg
1 tablespoon melted shortening
1 tablespoon sugar
2 teaspoons crushed dried sage
1/2 teaspoon salt
1/4 teaspoon baking soda
2 1/2 cups flour

Combine sugar, sage, salt, baking soda and flour. Dissolve yeast in 1/4 cup warm water. Beat egg and cottage cheese together until smooth. Add melted shortening and yeast. Add flour mixture slowly to egg mixture, beating well after each addition until a stiff dough is formed.

Cover dough with cloth and put in warm place until double in bulk (about 1 hour). Punch dough down, knead for one minute and place in well-greased pan. Cover and let rise for 40 minutes.

Bake in a 350-degree oven for 50 minutes. Brush top with melted shortening and sprinkle with crushed, roasted pine nuts or coarse salt.

Fry Bread
4 cups white flour
1/2 teaspoon salt
1 tablespoon baking powder

Combine all ingredients. Add about 1 1/2 cups lukewarm water and knead until dough is soft but not sticky. Shape dough into balls the size of a small peach. Shape into patties by hand; dough should be about 1/2 inch thick.

Make a small hole in the center of the round.
Fry one at a time in about 1 inch of hot lard or shortening in a heavy pan. Brown on both sides. Drain on paper towels and serve hot with honey or jam.

Corn Pone
A standard pone recipe is:
1 cup corn meal
1 teaspoon salt
¾ cup boiling water
1 tablespoon lard or fat

Combine the meal and salt, while blending gradually add water. Melt the fat in the baking pan. After pan is greased, pour surplus into the mixture and blend. The mix should not be more than one inch thick in the baking pan to start with. It will rise very little. (To make it rise like corn bread, 2 tsp of baking powder would be needed.) The pone will develop a rich, brown crunchy crust. In this modern day it would take about 50 to 60 minutes in a 350 degree oven.

Corn Cakes
Fried on a griddle, these cakes were served with butter as bread or with sorghum molasses as pan cakes.

1 egg, beaten slightly
1 cup corn meal
½ cup flour
1 tsp. salt
1 cup hot water (or milk)
1 tablespoon fat or lard
1 tsp. sugar

Mix dry ingredients, then stir in the others. Drop or pour on hot, greased surface. Fry to a golden brown on both sides.

Southern Spoon Bread
Stir together:
1 cup yellow corn meal
1 ½ teaspoon baking powder
½ tsp. salt
In greased (one-quart size) casserole pour:
2 eggs (beaten)
2 tablespoons butter (melted)
In medium-sized pan heat:
2 ¼ cups milk (stir to avoid scorching)

As it starts boiling, sprinkle in the dry ingredients, stirring vigorously with wooden spoon. Cook and stir for 2 to 3 minutes, as it thickens, mix with eggs in casserole. Bake at 425 degrees for 45 minutes. Serve from casserole with spoon. Add butter.

Native Fry Bread
Ingredients:
2 cups flour
3 teaspoons baking powder
1 teaspoon salt
1/2 cup dry milk
1 egg
1 cup warm water

Mix the dry ingredients together, mix the egg and the water, add to the dry mixture. Add flour or water to adjust mixture to a very soft dough mixture. Put dough on a well floured board. Roll out to about a 1 inch thickness. Let set for about 15 minutes. Cut into whatever size you would like. Batter makes about 25 pieces. Deep fry in hot oil, just enough to brown on each side. Put on a paper towel to get some of the top oil off the bread.

Blackfeet Fry Bread
4 cups flour
1 tablespoon powdered milk
1 tablespoon baking powder
1 teaspoon salt
1 1/2 cups warm water
Oil for frying

Mix all dry ingredients thoroughly. Add water. Knead until soft, then set aside for one hour. Shape into small balls. Flatten each ball into a circle with or rolling pin or by hand. Fry in a skillet half-full of oil until golden brown on both sides.

Cherokee Fry Bread
1 cup flour
1/2 teaspoon salt
2 teaspoons baking powder
3/4 cup milk

Mix ingredients adding more flour if necessary to make a stiff dough. Roll out the dough on a floured board till very thin. Cut into strips 2 X 3 inches and drop in hot cooking oil. Brown on both sides. Serve hot with honey.

Chickasaw Fry Bread
2 cups sifted flour
1/2 teaspoon salt
4 teaspoon baking powder
1 egg
1/2 cup warm milk

Stir first three ingredients then stir in the beaten egg. Add milk to make the dough soft. Roll it out on floured bread board, knead lightly. Roll dough out to 1/2 inch thick. Cut into strips 2 X 3 inches and slit the center. Drop into hot cooking oil and brown on both sides. Serve hot.

Pumpkin Fry Bread
2 cups sifted flour
1/2 teaspoon salt
4 teaspoon baking powder
1 egg
1/2 cup warm milk
2 cups fresh pumpkin or 1-16oz. can pumpkin
1 tablespoon milk or water
3/4 cups brown sugar
1/4 teaspoon cinnamon
1/4 teaspoon nutmeg
1/4 teaspoon vanilla

Drop into hot cooking oil and brown on both sides. Serve hot with butter or powdered sugar.

Creek Fry Bread
2 cups flour
1 cup buttermilk
1 tablespoon baking powder
1/4 teaspoon salt

Sift flour, salt and baking powder then add milk and more flour to make dough stiff. Roll out onto floured bread board and cut into 4 X 4 squares with a slit in the center. Fry in hot cooking oil until golden brown. Drain on plate with paper towels.

Navajo Fry Bread #1
1 cup flour
1 teaspoon baking powder
1/4 cup powdered milk
1/4 teaspoon salt
warm water

Combine the ingredients and slowly add enough warm water to form dough. On a lightly floured surface, knead dough until it is smooth soft and not sticky. Cover and let rest 1 hour. Shape into small balls and pat into flat circles about 1/4-1/2 inch thick. Set aside.

In skillet, heat 1/2 inch vegetable oil. Brown dough circles on each side and drain on paper towels.

Serve with chile beans and your favorite taco toppings for "Navajo Tacos."

Navajo Fry Bread #2
3 cups unbleached flour, sifted
1/2 cup dry powdered milk
1 tablespoon baking powder
1/2 teaspoon salt
1/2 cup warm water or milk
2 quarts oil for deep frying

Combine the first 5 ingredients in a large mixing bowl and knead until smooth and soft, but not sticky. Depending on the altitude and humidity, you may need to adjust the liquid or the flour, so go slowly and balance accordingly. Be careful not to overwork the dough, or it will become tough and chewy. Brush a tablespoon of oil over the finished dough and allow it to rest 20 minutes to 2 hours in a bowl covered with a damp cloth. After the dough has rested, heat the oil in a broad, deep frying pan or kettle until it reaches a low boil (375°). Pull off egg-sized balls of dough and quickly roll, pull, and path them out into large, plate-sized rounds. They should be thin in the middle and about 1/4 inch thick at the edges. Carefully ease each piece of flattened dough into the hot, boiling oil, one at a time. Using a long-handled cooking fork or tongs, turn the dough one time. Allow about 2 minutes cooking time per side. When golden brown, lift from oil, shake gently to remove bulk of oil, and place on layered brown paper or paper towels to finish draining.

Serve hot with honey, jelly, fine powdered sugar, or various meat toppings.

Indian Crackers
1/2 cup shelled raw pinon nuts
1/2 cup shelled raw sunflower seeds
1/4 teaspoon salt

Grind nuts and seeds together very fine, add salt and form into small balls. Flatten carefully between palms into thin wafers. Wrap each wafer in soft corn husk or aluminum foil and bake in 350 oven for 40 to 50 minutes, testing to see that crackers are not too brown. These crackers are eaten as snacks or with soup.

Osage Fry Bread
4 cups all purpose flour
2 teaspoon salt
1 tablespoon and a half baking powder
1 tablespoon melted shortening
2 cups warm milk
Shortening for deep frying

Sift flour, salt and baking powder into bowl. Stir in shortening and milk. Knead the dough into a ball. Roll out dough on lightly floured board. Cut into diamond shapes and slice a slit in the center.

Heat shortening in deep fryer to 370 degrees. Fry 2 or 3 at a time until golden brown on both sides. Drain on paper towels.

Seminole Fry Bread
2 cups flour
3 teaspoon baking powder
1 teaspoon salt
1 cup milk

Mix flour, baking powder and salt. Add milk gradually making sure the dough is stiff. Put on floured bread board and pat it out with your hands until it is 1/2 inch thick. Cut into strips with a slit in the center. Fry in hot oil until both sides are golden brown.

Jalapeno Cornbread
1 cup cornmeal
1/3 cup all-purpose flour
1 tablespoon sugar optional
2 teaspoons double-acting baking powder
1/2 teaspoon baking soda
2 pc large eggs beaten
1 cup buttermilk

1/3 cup onions minced
1 cup creamed corn 8 ounce can
2 tablespoons green peppers minced
2 tablespoons jalapeno peppers chopped
1/2 cup cheddar cheese, shredded

Combine dry ingredients in mixing bowl. In a separate bowl add the beaten eggs and all the remaining ingredients, blending well. Add the two mixtures together and stir only until moistened. ?Use a heavy cast iron skillet if available; if not, use a 9-inch square baking dish. Grease the skillet or dish, pour in the mixture and bake in a preheated 350-degree oven for 30-35 minutes or until golden brown. Cool slightly and serve immediately.

Chestnut Bread
Ingredients for 5-6 servings:

1 peel one pound of chestnuts and scale to take off the inside skin. Add enough cornmeal to hold chestnuts together, mixing chestnuts and cornmeal with boiling water. Wrap in green fodder or green corn shucks, tying each bun securely with white twine. Place in a pot of boiling water and cook until done. Salt when eating if desired. Bean bread can be made the same way, but cook beans until tender before adding cornmeal. No salt should be added before or during cooking or the bread will crumble.

Acorn Bread
To make bread, you will need the following:

6 tablespoons cornmeal
1/2 cup cold water
1 cup boiling water
1 teaspoon salt
1 tablespoon butter
1 package active dry yeast
1/4 cup lukewarm water
1 cup mashed potatoes
2 cups all-purpose flour
2 cups finely ground leached acorn meal

Mix cornmeal with cold water, add boiling water and cook 2 minutes, stirring constantly. Add sale and butter and cool to lukewarm. Soften yeast in lukewarm water. Add remaining ingredients to corn mixture, along with yeast. Knead to a stiff dough. Dough will be sticky. Cover and let rise in warm place until doubled in bulk. Punch down, shape into two loaves, cover and let rise until doubled in bulk. Bake at 375 degrees F for 45 minutes.

Wild Sage Bread
1 package dry yeast
1 cup cottage cheese
1 egg
1 tablespoon melted shortening
1 tablespoon sugar
2 teaspoons crushed dried sage
1/2 teaspoon salt
1/4 teaspoon baking soda

2 1/2 cups flour

Combine sugar, sage, salt, baking soda and flour. Dissolve yeast in 1/4 cup warm water. Beat egg and cottage cheese together until smooth. Add melted shortening and yeast. Add flour mixture slowly to egg mixture, beating well after each addition until a stiff dough is formed.

Cover dough with cloth and put in warm place until double in bulk (about 1 hour). Punch dough down, knead for one minute and place in well-greased pan. Cover and let rise for 40 minutes.

Bake in a 350-degree oven for 50 minutes. Brush top with melted shortening and sprinkle with crushed, roasted pine nuts or coarse salt.

Cornbread
Sift the following ingredients together:
1 cup flour
¾ teaspoon baking soda
1 teaspoon salt
1 teaspoon baking powder
Add 1 ½ cups cornmeal.

Combine the following ingredients together:
2 eggs (well beaten)
2 tablespoons brown sugar
½ cup melted shortening

Add the eggs, sugar, and shortening to 1 ½ cups of buttermilk, then add to cornmeal mixture. Beat only until moist. Bake in a well-oiled pan or iron skillet at 450 degrees until golden brown.

Corn Cakes

Ingredients
cinnamon
1/3 cup water
1 cup pounded corn
honey

Directions
Pound hard corn until powder like. Pour in water. Sprinkle cinnamon and put in a small amount of honey. Make a type of patty cake. Melt butter in a small pan and cook until golden brown. (flip sides occasionally) Let cool and pour honey.

Bird Stuffing

Wild Rice
Green Onions
Celery
chopped nuts
chopped unpeeled apples
chopped dried fruit or berries
Sunflower seeds

Cook wild rice until nearly done. Fry green onions, celery, add chopped nuts, chopped unpeeled apples, chopped dried fruit or berries, sunflower seeds. Fold ingredients into the wild rice. Rice stuffing won't absorb fat the way bread stuffing does, but wild birds usually aren't very fat anyway, and neither are small chickens and most turkeys. Taste stuffing, add whatever seasonings you like with it. Use no conventional poultry seasonings, and remember too it doesn't need so much salt as regular rice, maybe none. Remember that one cup of raw rice cooks up to 4, and make an amount somewhat larger than needed to stuff your birds, because people like it a lot, so put some in a (covered) casserole too. Before you stuff wild birds wash inside and out very well with water that has baking soda and salt in it, then rinse. Then rub the cavity with butter.

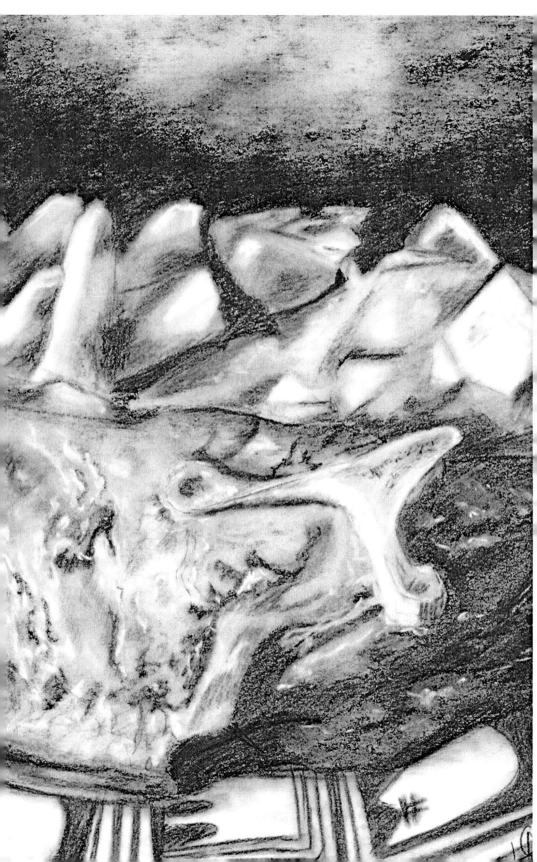

Meats and Main Dishes

Beef, Pork And Hominy Stew

1 1/2 lb lean pork ribs, cut into 1-inch pieces
1 lb cured bacon
1 lb flank steak, cut into 1-inch pieces
1 lb beef short ribs, cut between bones
3 sweet Italian sausage links, cut into 1 1/2-inch lengths
2 Spicy dried pork sausage links, cut into 1 1/2-inch lengths
3 quarts water
6 carrots, cut into 1/2-inch-thick rounds
1 1/2 lb butternut squash, peeled and cut into 3/4-inch cubes
1 large boiling potato, peeled and cut into 3/4-inch cubes
2 red bell peppers, cut into 3/4-inch pieces
1 tablespoon paprika
3 (15-oz) cans white hominy, rinsed
2 (16- to 19-oz) cans white beans, rinsed
1 tablespoon salt
1 tablespoon black pepper

Stir together meats and water in a 12-quart heavy pot and bring to a boil. Reduce heat and simmer, partially covered, stirring occasionally, 3 1/2 hours.

Add vegetables and paprika then simmer, partially covered, stirring occasionally, 30 minutes, or until vegetables are tender. Add hominy, beans, salt, and pepper and simmer, stirring occasionally, 15 minutes.

Rabbit Soup
leftover rabbit meat and bones
1 soup bone
1/4 lb salt pork
3 carrots, sliced
1 onion, quartered
1 clove garlic
1/4 teaspoon chopped parsley
1/4 teaspoon thyme
1 bay leaf
4 cups chicken broth
salt and pepper
1 cup diced potatoes
1/2 cup diced celery
1/2 cup diced carrots

Remove all meat from rabbit bones and set meat aside. in a kettle, combine rabbit bones and soup bone and salt pork. Add sliced carrots, onion, garlic, parsley, thyme and bay leaf. Cover with water and simmer until almost dry.

Add chicken broth and simmer 15 minutes. Strain broth and adjust the seasoning to taste. Discard bones and seasoning vegetables.

Add potatoes to broth and simmer until tender. Add celery and carrots and cook 20 minutes longer. Add rabbit meat. Heat thoroughly and serve.

Comanche Stew
5 lbs beef, stewing
3 lbs bacon or salt pork
1 hen (approx. 4 lb)
12 1/2 cups tomatoes, canned
7 1/2 cups corn kernels
7 1/2 cups green peas
2 pints oysters
4 onions, large
3 chile ancho
8 lbs potatoes
salt to taste
pepper to taste
cayenne pepper to taste

Optional Additional Meats:
Rabbit
Game birds
Squirrel

Put all meat and the chiles in a stew kettle in enough boiling water to cover, and cook for 2 to 2 and 1/2 hours.

Add potatoes, tomatoes, and onions, and cook for about half an hour before adding the corn and peas. The oysters should be added about 15 minutes before the stew is removed from the stove, and may be left out entirely. Total cooking time about four hours.

Seminole Roast Rabbit
1 skinned and dressed rabbit
1/2 cup vegetable oil
1 cup all-purpose flour
Salt and pepper to taste
Corn Stuffing

Heat oven to 425-degrees F.

Pat the rabbit dry and stuff with the corn stuffing. Place a piece of foil into the opening. Truss rabbit with a string, by tying together the hind and front legs.

Brush rabbit with oil. Let oil drip off. Mix together flour, salt and pepper and sprinkle the rabbit generously with the flour mixture. Place on rack on its side in a roasting pan.

Roast in oven for 10 minutes; reduce heat to 350-F and roast for 1 1/2 hours, turning frequently. Baste rabbit with pan drippings and oil 3-4 times during roasting.

Remove from oven and let rest before carving for about 10 minutes.

Cured Venison
3 lbs salt
4 tablespoons cinnamon
5 tablespoons black pepper
4 tablespoons allspice
Fresh venison meat

Cut meat into strips 12 inches long, 2 inches thick and 4 wide. Remove all membrane so curing mixture will adhere to moist meat.

Mix dried ingredients together thoroughly and rub well into every surface of strips, dusting on more. Thread each strip on string and hang in a cool, dry place out of the sun, not near artificial heat. Needs to be hung in this manner for one month, then is ready for eating without cooking as a jerked meat.

Buffalo Stew (Tanka-me-a-lo)
2 Stalks of celery, cut 1 inch long
1 Can stewed tomatoes
2 lbs of buffalo stew meat, cut into 1 inch cubes
4 Quarts water
2 lbs of red or white potatoes... (not russets)
1 Cup barley

Directions
Brown the buffalo cubes on high heat until seared about 3 min Add 4 quarts of water, potatoes and carrots and boil until Veggies are tender. Add stewed tomatoes and celery and barley cook an additional 5 minutes.
Remove from fire and place into baking dish.
Bake at 425 degrees for 30 minutes.
Remove from oven and enjoy.

Grilled Salmon
Ingredients
Dab of salt & pepper
Salmon

Directions
Catch and clean a salmon and fillet it.

Stovetop:
get a pan real hot and put a dab of oil.
lay the salmon on it salt & pepper it and put a lid on it.
check it out and flip over before it burns.

Fire Baked Fish
Ingredients
Salt and Pepper
1 Big Fish (Salmon, Trout, Perch)
Butter
Lemon Slices

Directions
Gut and scale the fish.
Place lemon in the fish and rub all over with butter.
Sprinkle with salt and pepper and wrap in a big piece of tinfoil.

Bake on a smooth flat rock really close to the fire (but not in it!).

Use some long sticks to get it out.

Note: The amount of time it takes to cook varies depending on the size of fish and how close it is to the fire. Just keep checking it, it will be done when the flesh flakes easily with a fork.

Spicy Taino Guanaho (Wild Turkey)

Ingredients
1 4-pound Turkey
1/2 teaspoon ground cumin seeds
8 garlic cloves, peeled
1/2 cup olive oil
1 teaspoon rock salt
2 teaspoons paprika
1 tablespoon chopped fresh oregano
3 chopped green onions
1 teaspoon black peppercorns
2 medium tomatoes, chopped
4 small hot chili peppers
1 tablespoon chopped fresh cilantro
1 teaspoon minced fresh gingerroot
Garnish: lemon wedges
1/4 teaspoon saffron threads

Directions
Wash the turkey parts, pat dry and remove the skin. Place in a deep square pan and set aside. In the belly of a mortar, combine garlic, salt, oregano, and black peppercorns. Press down with the pestle until garlic is crushed and peppercorns are cracked, then add the chili peppers, minced ginger, and saffron threads. Slowly pound the mixture until achieving a paste and incorporate the oil slowly. At the same time, stir with a spoon to break down the paste.

Spread the mixture evenly over the turkey parts, lifting the chicken pieces to ensure distribution of the marinade to the bottom of the turkey parts. Sprinkle all parts with paprika. Cover and refrigerate overnight. If no mortar and pestle is available, execute the steps in a blender set on low speed until all the ingredients are coarsely chopped, then remove the canister, add the oil and shake or stir to break down the paste and blend the ingredients.

In a preheated deep skillet, over low-to-medium heat, arrange marinated turkey pieces side by side and brown the turkey on all sides. Spread the chopped onions, chopped tomatoes, and drizzle the burgundy over the chicken parts.

Cover and finish cooking on low heat for approximately 35 minutes. Remove from heat and sprinkle chopped cilantro on the chick prior to serving. You may serve directly from the skillet.

Good Deer
Ingredients
4 cloves fresh garlic, finely minced
1 qtr teaspoon Finely ground red hot pepper
1qtr teaspoon Oregano
1 qtr teaspoon Basil
1 to 2 lb. Ground
1 chopped onion
Salt to taste after cooking
1 bag of wide egg noodles.

Directions

First, using a cast iron skillet of appropriate size , and enough olive oil to cover the bottom, slowly simmer the deer meat to brown.

While it is browning, add all other ingredients except the noodles which should be happily boiling in water in their own kettle.

When the garlic /onion is sautéed to tender, add some water to the skillet to help blend the flavors and let it s l o w l e y cook down, fending off those who would eat before it is ready.

Adjust spice to taste after it has cooked down. Serve over the drained cooked noodles.

Baked Quail With Mushrooms
1 cup all-purpose flour
1 teaspoon salt
1/2 teaspoon pepper
6 each quail; cleaned
2 tablespoons butter
1/2 pounds fresh mushrooms; sliced
1/2 cup butter
1/4 cup plus 1 tbsp all-purpose flour
2 cups chicken broth
1/2 cup sherry
1 hot cooked wild rice

Combine 1/3 cup flour, salt, and pepper. Dredge quail in flour mixture, and set aside. Melt 2 tablespoons butter in a large skillet; add mushrooms, and sauté 4 minutes. Remove mushrooms from skillet; set aside. Melt 1/2 cup butter in skillet; brown quail on both sides. Remove quail to a 1-1/2 quart casserole. Add 1/4 cup plus 1 tablespoon flour to drippings in skillet; cook 1 minute, stirring constantly. Gradually add chicken broth and sherry; cook over medium heat, stirring constantly, until gravy is thickened and bubbly. Stir in mushrooms. Pour mushroom gravy over quail. Cover and bake at 350F for 1 hour. Serve over wild rice Notes: 'Southern Living' Yield: 6 servings

Venison And Wild Rice Stew
3 1/2 lbs. shoulder of venison, cut into 2" cubes
2 teaspoon salt
pepper to taste
2 quarts water
2 large onions; peeled and quartered
1 1/2 cups wild rice, washed in cold water

Put venison, water, and onions in a large pot; simmer uncovered for 3 hours.

Add salt, pepper, wild rice. Cover and simmer for 20 minutes.

Stir well; simmer uncovered for another 20 minutes, or until rice is tender and most of liquid is absorbed.

Venison Acorn Stew
To make venison stew, you will need the following:
2 lbs venison, cut up
1 Cup finely ground acorn meal

Cover venison with water in pot or basket; Add hot rocks to simmer until meat almost falls apart. Remove meat from broth and chop into fine pieces. Return to pot with liquid and stir in acorn meal. Serve hot.

Meatless Chili
1 cup dried pinto or kidney beans
3 cups water
1 tablespoon vegetable oil
2 cups chopped onion
1 green bell pepper, chopped
2 cups chopped tomatoes
1 6-ounce can no-salt added tomato paste
3/4 cup water
3 tablespoons chili powder
1 tablespoon cider vinegar
2 teaspoons minced garlic
1 teaspoon oregano
1 teaspoon cumin

1/2 teaspoon ground pepper
1 bay leaf

Place beans and 3 cups of water in saucepan. Bring to boil and cook 2 minutes. Do not drain. Set aside for 1 hour, then return beans to heat, adding water to cover if necessary. Simmer for 1 hour, or until beans are tender. Drain and set aside.

Heat oil in a large, deep skillet or stockpot over medium-high heat. Add onion and bell pepper. Cook until onion is translucent. Add beans and remaining ingredients. Bring to a boil. Reduce heat and simmer 1 1/2 hours, stirring occasionally. Remove bay leaf

Baked Quail With Mushrooms
1 cup all-purpose flour
1 teaspoon salt
1/2 teaspoon pepper
6 each quail; cleaned
2 tablespoons butter
1/2 pounds fresh mushrooms; sliced
1/2 cup butter
1/4 cup plus 1 tbsp all-purpose flour
2 cups chicken broth
1/2 cup sherry
1 hot cooked wild rice

Combine 1/3 cup flour, salt, and pepper. Dredge quail in flour mixture, and set aside. Melt 2 tablespoons butter in a large skillet; add mushrooms, and sauté 4 minutes. Remove mushrooms from skillet; set aside. Melt 1/2 cup butter in skillet; brown quail on both sides. Remove quail to a 1-1/2 quart casserole. Add 1/4 cup plus 1 tablespoon flour to drippings in skillet; cook 1 minute, stirring constantly. Gradually add chicken broth and sherry; cook over medium heat, stirring constantly, until gravy is thickened and bubbly. Stir in mushrooms. Pour mushroom gravy over quail. Cover and bake at 350F for 1 hour. Serve over wild rice Notes: 'Southern Living' Yield: 6 servings

Baked Trout
4 pieces trout fillets, rinsed and dried (about 1-1/4 lbs. total)
2 tbs. lime juice
3/4 pc medium tomato, chopped
1/4 pc medium onion, chopped
1/4 tsp. olive oil
2 tbs. cilantro, chopped
1/8 tsp. salt
1/8 tsp. black pepper

Preheat oven to 350°F. Place fish fillets in baking dish. In separate dish, mix remaining ingredients together. Pour over fish and bake for 15 to 20 minutes or until fish flakes easily with a fork.

Bison Chili
1 lb. ground bison
1 pc medium onion, chopped
1 15 oz. can pinto beans, rinsed and drained
2 16 oz. cans peeled tomatoes
1/2 cup water
2 teaspoon chili powder
1/2 teaspoon ground cumin
1/2 teaspoon salt
1/2 teaspoon ground pepper
1/4 cup fresh cilantro, chopped

In a non-stick skillet, sauté the Ground Bison and onion until the meat is browned and the onion is tender. Add the pinto beans, tomatoes, water and seasonings. Cover and simmer for 1 hour, adding more water if chili becomes too thick. Add chopped cilantro and simmer an additional 10 minutes. Spoon into bowls and garnish with grated cheese or diced jalapeno peppers. Yield: serves 4.

Bison Porcupine Meatballs
1 lb. ground bison
1/4 cup uncooked long-grain rice
1 slightly beaten egg
1tablespoon snipped parsley
2 tablespoons. finely chopped onion
1/2teaspoon salt
dash of pepper

1 10 oz. can condensed tomato soup
1/2 cup water
1 teaspoon Worcestershire sauce

Combine Ground Bison, rice, egg, parsley, onion, salt, pepper and only 1/4 cup condensed tomato soup. Mix thoroughly; shape into about 20 small meatballs and place in skillet. Mix remaining soup, water and Worcestershire sauce and pour over meatballs. Bring to boil; reduce heat; cover and simmer 40 minutes, stirring often.

Buffalo Rice Casserole
1 pound ground buffalo meat
1 cup cooked wild rice
1/4 cup chopped onion
1/4 cup finely chopped celery
1/4 cup chopped poblano pepper
1 can cream of mushroom soup or cream of celery

Brown buffalo meat and drain. Sauté onions, pepper, and celery; drain. Mix all ingredients together and pour into casserole dish. Bake for 30 minutes or until bubbly at 350 degrees.

Catfish Fillets With Cornbread Stuffing
1-1/2 lbs catfish fillets
2 tablespoons butter or margarine
1 pc medium cooking apple, cored and chopped
1/2 cup sliced celery
1 (6oz) package seasoned cornbread stuffing mix
seasonings, paprika, salt and pepper, to taste

Rinse and pat dry the fish with a paper towel. Season Catfish with the seasonings. In a large nonstick skillet, cook fish in hot butter for 3 minutes, add chopped apple and celery. cook for 3 or 4 minutes more or until fish flakes easily when tested with a fork. Remove catfish, and keep warm. Add 1 1/2 cups water to the same skillet, bring to a boil. Stir in dry stuffing mix and seasoning packet that sometimes comes with the mix. cover and let stand 5 minutes serve the stuffing with the fish.

Garlic Stuffed Buffalo Steaks
2 pieces buffalo steaks (rib eyes, new York strip, top sirloin, or file
1 tbs. olive oil
1 tsp. pepper
1/4 cup garlic, very finely chopped
1/2 cup green onions, thinly sliced

In a small nonstick skillet, heat oil over medium-low heat until hot. Add garlic. Cook and stir 4-5 minutes or until tender, but not browned. Add onions. Continue cooking and stirring 4-5 minutes or until onions are tender. Season with salt and pepper; cool completely. Meanwhile with a sharp knife, cut a pocket in each bison steak. Start 1/2 inch from one long side of steak and cut horizontally through center of steak to within 1/2 inch of each side. Spread half of garlic mixture inside each steak pocket. Secure opening with wooden toothpicks. Set oven to BROIL. Preheat broiler. Position broiler pan so surface of steak is 5 inches from heat source. Broil until top side is brown approximately 8-10 minutes. Turn and brown other side for 5-7 minutes for medium doneness.

Green Chile Chicken Corn Chowder
1 tbsp extra virgin olive oil
1 (12 oz) package pre-cooked jalapeno chicken sausage^
1 cup chopped onion
1 cup diced red bell pepper
4 cloves garlic (minced)
1 tsp ground cumin
1/2 tsp cayenne (ground red pepper)
4 cups fat-free low-sodium chicken broth
1/2 cup canned green chilies
2 cups baby red or Yukon gold potatoes (scrubbed & chopped)
3 cups frozen whole-kernel corn
1/2 cup all-purpose flour
2 cups 1% milk
1 1/2 cups shredded sharp cheddar cheese
salt and pepper (to taste)
^ (sliced or chopped into bite-sized pieces)

Heat the olive oil in a large pot over medium-high heat. Add chicken sausage, onion, bell pepper, garlic and sauté 5 minutes. Add cumin, and cayenne pepper into the mixture, and sauté for 1 minute. Add broth, green chiles and potatoes and bring to boil. Cover, reduce heat to low, and simmer until potatoes are tender (10-15 minutes). Add corn and stir well. Raise stove heat to medium. Place flour in a bowl and gradually add milk, stirring with a whisk until blended. Add flour mixture to soup and cook over medium heat until thick (about 15 minutes), stirring frequently. Stir in cheese, salt, and pepper and serve with bread.

Grilled Cornish Game Hens With Nopales And Pine Nuts

2 tablespoons unsalted butter
1 tablespoon honey
2 teaspoons chili powder
1 teaspoon Spanish paprika
1 teaspoon lime juice
1 teaspoon orange juice
salt and freshly ground black pepper
2 1 1/4 lbs Cornish game hens, halved length wise
1 whole nopali, cut into small squares
3 ounces olive oil
3 ounces grated parmesan cheese
1 ounce pine nuts, roasted and chopped

Preheat the grill. In a small saucepan, melt butter and mix with honey, chili powder, and paprika. Remove the pan from the heat, stir in the lime and orange juices, and season with salt and pepper. Rinse the pieces of game hen, pat them dry and season with salt. Grill the hen halves, skin sides down, for 20 minutes. Turn halves over with metal tongs and baste with the butter mixture. Cook for 20 more minutes or until a thermometer inserted sideways in the center of the breast the reads 160°F. While the hens cook, put the nopali in a grill pan, mix with olive oil, and season with salt and pepper. Cook the cactus on the grill until they are soft and a little brown. Transfer nopali to a mixing bowl and season with parmesan cheese and pine nuts.

Grilled Cornish Game Hens With Nopales And Pine Nuts
2 tablespoons unsalted butter
1 tablespoon honey
2 teaspoons chili powder
1 teaspoon Spanish paprika
1 teaspoon lime juice
1 teaspoon orange juice
salt and freshly ground black pepper
2 1 1/4 lbs Cornish game hens, halved length wise
1 whole nopali, cut into small squares
3 ounces olive oil
3 ounces grated parmesan cheese
1 ounce pine nuts, roasted and chopped

Preheat the grill. In a small saucepan, melt butter and mix with honey, chili powder, and paprika. Remove the pan from the heat, stir in the lime and orange juices, and season with salt and pepper. Rinse the pieces of game hen, pat them dry and season with salt. Grill the hen halves, skin sides down, for 20 minutes. Turn halves over with metal tongs and baste with the butter mixture. Cook for 20 more minutes or until a thermometer inserted sideways in the center of the breast the reads 160°F. While the hens cook, put the nopali in a grill pan, mix with olive oil, and season with salt and pepper. Cook the cactus on the grill until they are soft and a little brown. Transfer nopali to a mixing bowl and season with parmesan cheese and pine nuts.

Maple Salmon
1/4 cup maple syrup (the real thing no imitations)
1 teaspoon salt
1 clove garlic, minced
1/4 teaspoon garlic salt
1/8 teaspoon black pepper
2-4 pieces salmon fillets

In bowl mix all together except the fish. Place salmon in shallow baking dish & coat all sides with sauce. Cover & marinate 30 minutes. Preheat oven to 400 F (200 C). Uncover dish & place in hot oven for about 20 minutes until fish flakes.

Native Skillet Chicken
2 cubes chicken bouillon
1 cup water
1 package smoky link sausages
2-4 chicken breasts (diced)
1 1/2 cups cooked wild and brown rice
1 pc medium tomato, chopped
1 pc medium onion, chopped

1 pc medium poblano pepper, chopped
1/2 t. thyme
1/2 pc jalapeno
1 pkg. frozen peas

Dissolve chicken bouillon in 1 cup water. In a large skillet, brown sausages for 5 minutes. Add chicken breasts and brown 5 minutes. Add all other ingredients, including bouillon, and simmer 5 minutes. Turn off heat and let sit 5 minutes.

Rabbit Hot Pot Casserole
1 pc rabbit, dressed
4 pieces carrots, peeled and sliced
4 pieces potatoes, peeled and sliced
1 package onion soup mix
2 1/2 cups hot water

Cut rabbit into serving pieces and wash well. Blanch rabbit by putting it into a saucepan. Cover with water and bring to a boil. Remove rabbit from the saucepan and place in a greased casserole dish. Cover rabbit with the carrots and potatoes. Mix soup with the hot water and pour over vegetables. Cover and bake at 350 F for 2 hours.

Native American Rabbit Pot
1 pc young rabbit
1 tablespoon fat,
1 cup broth or water with chicken
1 bouillon cube
1/4 cup lemon juice
3/4 cup orange juice
1/2 c mushrooms, chopped,
1 tablespoon parsley, chopped,
1 pinch ginger
1/2 teaspoon salt
1/4 teaspoon pepper
2 pieces green peppers, chopped.

Cut up the rabbit and brown pieces in fat in a heavy pot. Add broth and other ingredients, season with salt, pepper and ginger. Cover and cook slowly until tender.

Native Baked Buffalo Steak Reservation Style
2 pounds thick round buffalo steak
lard
salt and pepper
2 cups flour
2 teaspoon baking powder
1 teaspoon salt
1 cup cream (half and half)
2 pieces egg yolks, beaten
1 tablespoon Worcestershire sauce
1 teaspoon chili powder
1 teaspoon cumin
1 teaspoon onion powder
2 pieces egg whites, stiffly beaten

Brown buffalo on both sides in shortening. Salt and pepper to taste. Sift dry ingredients together and add egg yolks, half and half, Worcestershire sauce. Mix well and fold in egg white. Place steak in a baking pan with a little of the grease from the skillet. Pour the flour mixture over the steak. Bake about 1 1/2 hours at 350 or until steak is tender. Unusual way and easy to serve a very old reservation tough steak.

Native Buffalo Steak And Beans
1 tablespoon all-purpose flour
1/2 teaspoon chili powder
1/4 teaspoon salt
1/8 teaspoon ground cumin
1/8 teaspoon pepper
1/2 pound boneless buffalo steak, cut into; 1-inch cubes
1 tablespoon vegetable oil
3/4 cup thinly sliced celery
1 pc medium onion, chopped
1/2 cup water
1/4 cup chili sauce
1 pc medium carrot, cut into 1/2-inch slices
1 pc small green pepper, cut into 1 1/2; -inch strips
3/4 cup kidney beans, rinsed and drained
hot cooked wild rice

In a re-sealable plastic bag, combine the first five ingredients. Add the steak; shake to coat. In a skillet, cook steak in oil until browned on all sides; drain. Add the celery, onion, water and chili sauce. Bring to a boil. Reduce heat; cover and simmer for 30 minutes. Add carrot; cover and simmer for 15 minutes. Stir in green pepper and beans.

Cover and simmer 10 minutes longer or until meat and vegetables are tender. Serve over rice or on fry bread if desired.

Venison Stew
2 tablespoons cooking oil
2 lbs. venison stew meat
3 large onions, coarsely chopped
2 garlic cloves, crushed
1tablespoons Worcestershire sauce
1 bay leaf
1teaspoon dried oregano
1teaspoon salt
1 teaspoon pepper
3 cups water
7 pieces potatoes, peeled and quartered
1 lb. carrots, cut into 1-inch pieces
1/4 cup all-purpose flour
1/4 cup cold water

Heat oil in Dutch oven. Brown meat. Add onions, garlic, Worcestershire sauce, bay leaf, oregano, salt and pepper. Simmer, covered, 1-1/2 to 2 hours until meat is tender. Add potatoes and carrots. Continue to cook until vegetables are tender, 30-45 minutes.

Mix flour and water; stir into stew. Cook and stir until thickened and bubbly. Remove bay leaf.

Salmon Patties

1 (15.5oz.) can Alaska salmon
3 slices bread (torn into small pieces)
1/3 cup minced onion
¼ cup milk
2 eggs
2 T. minced parsley
1 tablespoon lemon juice
¼ tsp. salt
¼ tsp. dill
Dash pepper
2 tbsp. oil and flour

Drain the salmon, reserving 2 tbsp. of the liquid. Combine the salmon with the bread pieces, onion, milk, eggs, parsley, salt, dill, and pepper; mix thoroughly. Shape into 6 patties and coat each with flour lightly. Pan-fry on both sides in oil until golden brown.

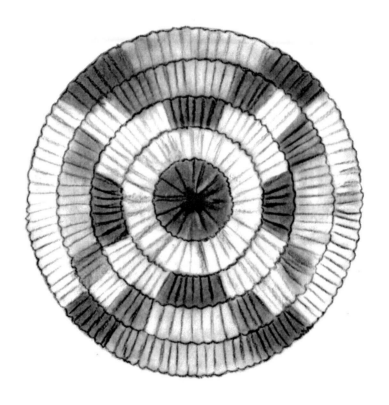

How to Avoid Food Poisoning
In Home-Cooked Foods

Proper cooking and handling of food can reduce the risk of food poisoning. Salmonella and other bacteria can be present in meat and poultry products without giving off any telltale signs, like bad taste or bad smell, so it's important to prevent these bacteria from spreading or multiplying to dangerous levels. The basic rule is: keep hot foods hot and cold foods cold. Here are some recommendations for avoiding trouble:

- Don't thaw meat or poultry on the kitchen counter. Instead, thaw it overnight in the refrigerator, or put frozen package in a watertight plastic bag under cold water, changing the water often.

- Don't leave hot food out for more than two hours. Even in a chafing dish, the food often isn't kept hot enough to discourage bacteria growth.

- Don't cool leftovers on the kitchen counter. It's safer to put them straight into the refrigerator.

- Pick up perishable foods last when grocery shopping, and get them home and into the refrigerator quickly.

- Repeated handling can introduce bacteria into food. Leave food in the original store wrapper when refrigerating.

- Keep your refrigerator set at 40 degrees or lower.

Cook meat and poultry thoroughly to kill bacteria. Most food poisoning bacteria are killed at cooking temperatures between 165 degrees and 212 degrees. Use a meat thermometer, instead into the thickest part, away from the bone or fat.

Freeze Now – Heat Later

One of the best things about modern times that the good old days lacked is refrigeration, and the convenience of cooking food ahead of time, freezing it, and then being able to just heat it up when we need it. Here are some tips on using your freezer to keep foods tasting delicious and staying fresh:

- Always chill dishes freezing them, since a still-warm dish takes longer to freeze and allows the formation of ice crystals that change the color, taste, and texture of the food.

- Ceramic, metal, or glass baking dishes may be used to freeze prepared foods if they are tightly covered. Use packaging materials that are moisture proof, reasonably airtight, and durable. Heavy aluminum foil, freezer paper or bags, poly wrap, and strong plastic containers protect foods from freezer burn.

- Leave about half an inch of space (especially for foods with a sauce) so foods will have room to expand while freezing. When storing food in bags, press out excess air before sealing.

- Before you freeze, label each package with the contents, date prepared, and the number of servings.

- Don't freeze emulsified sauces such as hollandaise sauce; they will curdle and separate. Cream sauces are also risky to freeze, and gelatin or whipped-cream desserts don't freeze successfully.

- Be sure that your freezer is cold enough. Frozen foods held at 0 degrees or lower retain their quality longer.

Suggested Maximum Home-Storage Periods to Maintain Good Quality in Purchased Frozen Foods

Food	Approximate holding period at 0 degrees Fahrenheit

Fruits and Vegetables

	Months
Fruits, fruit juice concentrates	12
Vegetables	8

Baked Goods

Bread and yeast rolls:	
White Bread	3
Cinnamon Rolls	2
Plain Rolls	3
Cakes:	
Chocolate layer	4
Pound or Yellow	6
Fruit	12
Pies (unbaked):	
Apple and other fruit	8

Meat

Beef:	
Hamburger	4
Roasts and Steaks	12
Lamb:	
Patties (ground meat)	4
Roasts	9
Pork, cured:	2
Pork, fresh:	
Chops	4
Roasts	8
Veal:	
Cutlets, chops, and roasts	9
Cooked meat:	
Meat dinners and pies	3

Suggested Maximum Home-Storage Periods to Maintain Good Quality in Purchased Frozen Foods

Food	Approximate holding period at 0 degrees Fahrenheit

Poultry

	Months
Chicken:	
Cut-up	9
Whole	12
Duck or goose, whole:	6
Turkey:	
Cut-up	6
Whole	12
Cooked chicken or turkey dinners:	6

Fish and Shellfish

Fish Fillets:	
Cod, Flounder, Haddock, Halibut, Pollack	6
Mullet, Ocean Perch, Sea Trout, Striped Bass	3
Salmon steaks	2
Whiting, drawn	4
Shellfish:	
Clams, shucked	3
Oysters, shucked	4
Crabmeat:	
Dungeness	3
King	10
Shrimp:	12
Cooked fish and shellfish:	3

Frozen Desserts

Ice Cream or Sherbet	1

Cooking Tips

1. After stewing a chicken, cool in broth before cutting into chunks; it will have twice the flavor.
2. To slice meat into thin strips, as for stir-fry dishes, partially freeze it so it will slice more easily.
3. A roast with the bone in it will cook faster than a boneless roast. The bone carries the heat to the inside more quickly
4. When making a roast, place a dry onion soup mix in the bottom of your roaster pan. After removing the roast, add 1 can of mushroom soup and you will have good brown gravy.
5. For a juicier hamburger, add cold water to the beef before grilling (1/2 cup to 1 lb. of meat).
6. To freeze meatballs, place them on a cookie sheet until frozen. Place in plastic bags. They will stay separated so that you may remove as many as you want.
7. To keep cauliflower white while cooking, add a little milk to the water.
8. When boiling corn, add sugar to the water instead of salt. Salt will toughen the corn.
9. To ripen tomatoes, put them in a brown paper bag in a dark pantry, and they will ripen overnight.
10. To keep celery crisp, stand it upright in a pitcher of cold, salted water and refrigerate.
11. When cooking cabbage, place a small tin cup or a can half full of vinegar on stove near the cabbage. It will absorb the odor.
12. Potatoes soaked in salt water for 20 minutes before baking will cook more rapidly.
13. Let raw potatoes stand in cold water for at least a half-hour before frying in order to improve the crispness of French-fried potatoes. Dry potatoes thoroughly before adding to oil.

14. Use greased muffin tins as molds when baking stuffed green peppers.
15. A few drops of lemon juice in water will whiten boiled potatoes.
16. Buy mushrooms before they "open". When stems and caps are attached firmly, mushrooms are truly fresh.
17. Do not use metal bowls when mixing salads. Use wood, glass, or china.
18. Lettuce keeps better if you store it in the refrigerator without washing it. Keep the leaves dry. Wash lettuce the day you are going to use it.
19. Do not use baking soda to keep vegetables green. It destroys Vitamin C.
20. Do not despair if you over-salt gravy. Stir in some instant mashed potatoes to repair the damage. Just add a little more liquid in order to offset the thickening.
21. A leaf of lettuce dropped into the pot absorbs the grease from the top of soup.   Remove the lettuce and throw it away as soon as it has served its purpose.
22. To prevent splashing when frying meat, sprinkle a little salt into the pan before putting in the fat.
23. When bread is baking, a small dish of water in the oven will help to keep the crust from getting hard.
24. Rinse a pan in cold water before scalding milk to prevent sticking.
25. When you are creaming butter and sugar together, it's a good idea to rinse the bowl with boiling water first. They'll cream faster.
26. Dip the spoon in hot water to measure shortening, butter, etc.; the fat will slip out more easily.
27. Using a can opener that leaves a smooth edge, remove both ends from a flat can (the size that tuna is usually packed in) and you have a perfect mold for poaching eggs.
28. When preparing to bake biscuits, use the divider from an ice tray. Shape the dough to conform to the size of

the try, and press divider on dough. After baking the biscuits will separate at dividing lines.

29. Try using a thread instead of a knife when a cake is to be cut while it is still hot.

30. For lump-less gravies and creamy smooth sauces, use a small spring whisk and stir till all ingredients are blended.

Herbs & Spices

Acquaint yourself with herbs and spices. Add in small amounts, ¼ tsp. for every 4 servings. Crush dried herbs or snip fresh ones before using. Use 3 times more fresh herbs if substituting fresh for dried.

Basil – Sweet, warm flavor with an aromatic odor. Use whole or ground. Good with lamb, roast, stews, ground beef, vegetables, dressing and omelets.

Bay Leaves – Pungent flavor. Use whole leaf but remove before serving. Good in vegetable dishes, seafood, stews and pickles.

Caraway – Spicy taste and aromatic smell. Use in cakes, breads, soups, cheese and sauerkraut.

Chives – Sweet, mild flavor like that of onion. Excellent in salads, fish, soups and potatoes.

Cilantro – Use fresh. Excellent in salads, fish, chicken, rice, beans and Mexican dishes.

Curry Powder – Spices are combined to proper proportions to give a distinct flavor to meat, poultry, fish, and vegetables.

Dill – Both the seeds and leaves are flavorful. Leaves may be used as garnish or cooked with fish, soup, dressings, potatoes, and beans. Leaves or the whole plant may be used to flavor pickles.

Fennel – Sweet, hot flavor. Both the seeds and leaves are used. Use in small quantities in pies and baked goods. Leaves can be boiled with fish.

Ginger – A pungent root, this aromatic spice is sold fresh, dried or ground. Use in pickles, preserves, cakes, cookies, soups, and meat dishes.

Marjoram – May be used either dried or green. Use to flavor fish, poultry, omelets, lamb, stew, stuffing, and tomato juice.

Mint – Aromatic with a cool flavor. Excellent in beverages, fish, lamb, cheese, soup, peas, carrots, and fruit desserts.

Oregano – Strong, aromatic odor. Use whole or ground in tomato juice, fish, eggs, pizza, omelets, chili, stew, gravy, poultry, and vegetables.

Paprika – A bright red pepper, this spice is used in meat, vegetables, and soups or as a garnish for potatoes, salads, or eggs.

Parsley – Best when used fresh, but it can be used dried as a garnish or as a seasoning. Try in fish, omelets, soup, meat, stuffing, and mixed greens.

Rosemary – Very aromatic. It can be used either fresh or dried. It can be used to season fish, stuffing, beef, lamb, poultry, onions, eggs, bread, and potatoes. Great in dressings.

Saffron – Orange-yellow in color, this spice flavors or colors foods. Use in soup, chicken, rice, and breads.

Sage – Use either fresh or dried. The flowers are sometimes used in salads. May be used in tomato juice, fish, omelets, beef, poultry, stuffing, cheese spreads and breads.

Tarragon – Leaves have a pungent, hot taste. Use to flavor sauces, salads, fish, poultry, tomatoes, eggs, green beans, carrots, and dressings.

Thyme – Sprinkle leaves on fish or poultry before broiling or baking. Throw a few sprigs directly on coals shortly before meat is finished grilling.

Baking Breads
Hints for Baking Breads

1. Kneading the dough for 30 seconds after mixing improves the texture of baking powder biscuits.
2. Instead of shortening, use cooking or salad oil in waffles and hot cakes
3. When bread is baking, a small dish of water in the oven will help keep the crust from hardening.
4. Dip a spoon in hot water to measure shortening, butter, etc., and the fat will slip out more easily.
5. Small amounts of leftover corn may be added to pancake batter for variety.
6. To make bread crumbs, use the fine cutter of a food grinder and tie a large paper bag over the spout in order to prevent flying crumbs.
7. When you are doing any sort of baking you get better results if you remember to preheat your cookie sheet, muffin tins or cake pan.

Rules for Use of Leavening Agents

1. In simple flour mixtures, use 2 tsp. baking powder to leaven 1 cup flour. Reduce this amount by ½ tsp. for each egg used.
2. To 1 tsp. baking soda use 2 ¼ tsp. cream tarter, 2 cups freshly soured milk, or 1 cup molasses.
3. To substitute baking soda and an acid for baking powder, divide the amount of baking powder by 4. Take that as your measure and add acid according to rule 2.

Proportions of Baking Powder to Flour

Biscuits………………………………..	To 1 cup flour use 1 ¼ tsp. baking powder
Cake with oil………………………….	To 1 cup flour use 1 tsp. baking powder
Muffins………………………………..	To 1 cup flour use 1 ½ tsp. baking powder
Popovers………………………………	To 1 cup flour use 1 ¼ tsp. baking powder
Waffles………………………………..	To 1 cup flour use 1 ¼ tsp. baking powder

Proportions of Liquid to Flour

Drop Batter…………………………………..	To 1 cup liquid use 2 to 2 ½ cups flour
Pour Batter………………………………….	To 1 cup liquid use 1 cup flour
Soft Dough…………………………………..	To 1 cup liquid use 3 to 3 ½ cups flour
Stiff Dough………………………………….	To 1 cup liquid use 4 cups flour

Baking Breads
Time and Temperature Chart

Breads	Minutes	Temperature (degrees)
Biscuits………	12-15	…………………..400 – 450
Cornbread……	25-30	…………………..400 – 425
Gingerbread….	40-50	…………………..350 – 370
Loaf………… .	50-60	…………………..350 – 400
Nut Bread……	50-75	………………………….350
Popovers…… .	30-40	…………………..425 – 450
Rolls……… …	20-30	…………………..400 - 450

Baking Desserts

Perfect Cookies

Cookie dough that is to be rolled is much easier to handle after it has been refrigerated for 10 to 30 minutes. This keeps the dough from sticking, even though it may be soft. If not done, the soft dough may require more flour and too much flour makes cookies hard and brittle. Place on a floured board only as much dough as can be easily managed. Flour the rolling pin slightly and roll lightly to desired thickness. Cut shapes close together and add trimmings to the dough that needs to be rolled. Place pans or sheets in upper third of oven. Watch the cookies carefully while baking in order to avoid burned edges. When sprinkling sugar on cookies, try putting it into a salt shaker in order to save time.

Perfect Pies

1. Pie crust will be better and easier to make if all the ingredients are cool.
2. The lower crust should be placed in the pan so that it covers the surface smoothly. Air pockets beneath the surface will push the crust out of shape while baking.
3. Folding the top crust over the lower crust before crimping will keep juices in the pie.
4. In making custard pie, bake at a high temperature for about 10 minutes to prevent a soggy crust. Then finish baking at a low temperature.
5. When making cream pie, sprinkle crust with powdered sugar in order to prevent it from becoming soggy.

Perfect Cakes

1. Fill cake pans 2/3 full and spread batter into the corners and sides, leaving a slight hollow in the center.
2. Cake is done when it shrinks from the sides of the pan or if it springs back when touched lightly with the finger.
3. After removing a cake from the oven, place it on a rack for about 5 minutes. Then, the sides should be loosened and the cake turned out a rack in order to finish cooling.
4. Do not frost cakes until thoroughly cool.
5. Icing will remain where you put it if you sprinkle cake with powdered sugar first.

Baking Desserts
Time and Temperature Chart

Dessert	Time	Temperature (degrees)
Butter cake, layer....	20-40 min.	..........380 – 400
Butter cake, loaf......	40-60 min.	..........360 – 400
Cake, angel............	50-60 min.	..........300 – 360
Cake, fruit............	3-4 hrs.	..........275 – 325
Cake, sponge.........	40-60 min.	..........300 – 350
Cookies, molasses...	18-20 min.	..........350 – 375
Cookies, thin.........	10-12 min.	..........380 – 390
Cream Puffs...........	45-60 min.	..........300 – 350
Meringue..............	40-60 min.	..........250 – 300
Pie Crust..............	20-40 min.	..........400 - 500

Vegetables & Fruits

Vegetables	Cooking Method	Time
Artichokes	boiled	40 min.
	steamed	45 – 60 min.
Asparagus, tips	boiled	10 -15 min.
Beans, lima	boiled	20 – 40 min.
	steamed	60 min.
Beans, string	boiled	15 -35 min.
	steamed	60 min.
Beets, old	boiled or steamed	1 – 2 hrs.
Beets, young with skin	boiled	30 min.
	steamed	60 min.
	baked	70 – 90 min.
Broccoli, flowerets	boiled	5 – 10 min.
Broccoli, stems	boiled	20 – 30 min.
Brussels, sprouts	boiled	20 – 30 min.
Cabbage, chopped	boiled	10 – 20 min.
	steamed	25 min.
Carrots, cut across	boiled	8 – 10 min.
	steamed	40 min.
Cauliflower, flowerets	boiled	8 – 10 min.
Cauliflower, stem down	boiled	20 – 30 min.
Corn, green, tender	boiled	5 – 10 min.
	steamed	15 min.
	baked	20 min.
Corn on the cob	boiled	8 – 10 min.
	steamed	15 min.
Eggplant, whole	boiled	30 min.
	steamed	40 min.
	baked	45 min.
Parsnips	boiled	25 – 40 min.
	steamed	60 min.

	baked	60 – 75 min.
Peas, green	boiled or steamed	5 – 15 min.
Potatoes	boiled	20 – 40 min.
	steamed	60 min.
	baked	60 – 75 min.
Pumpkin or Squash	boiled	20 – 40 min.
	steamed	45 min.
	baked	60 min.
Tomatoes	boiled	5 – 15 min.
Turnips	boiled	25 – 40 min.

Vegetables & Fruits
Drying Time Table

Fruits	Sugar or Honey	Cooking Time
Apricots...................	¼ cup for each cup of fruit	.............About 40 min.
Figs........................	1 tablespoon for each cup of fruit	.............About 30 min.
Peaches..................	¼ cup for each cup fruit	.............About 45 min.
Prunes....................	2 T. for each cup of fruit	.............About 45 min.

Buying Fresh Vegetables

Artichokes: Look for compact, tightly closed heads with green, clean-looking leaves. Avoid those with leaves that are brown or separated.

Asparagus: Stalks should be tender and firm; tips should be close and compact. Choose the stalks with very little white; they are more tender. Use asparagus soon because it toughens rapidly.

Beans, Snap: Those with small seeds inside the pods are best. Avoid beans with dry-looking pods.

Broccoli, Brussels Sprouts, and Cauliflower: Flower clusters on broccoli and cauliflower should be tight and close together. Brussels sprouts should be firm and compact. Smudgy, dirty spots may indicate pests or disease.

Cabbage and Head Lettuce: Choose heads that are heavy for their size. Avoid cabbage with worm holes and lettuce with discoloration or soft rot.

Cucumbers: Choose long, slender cucumbers for best quality. May be dark or medium green, but yellow ones are undesirable.

Mushrooms: Caps should be closed around the stems. Avoid black or brown gills.

Peas and Lima Beans: Select pods that are well-filled but not bulging. Avoid dried, spotted, yellow, or flabby pods.

Buying Fresh Fruits

Bananas: Skin should be free of bruises and black or brown spots. Purchase them green and allow them to ripen at home at room temperature.

Berries: Select plump, solid berries with good color. Avoid stained containers which indicate wet or leaky berries. Berries with clinging caps, such as blackberries and raspberries, may be unripe. Strawberries without caps may be overripe.

Melons: In cantaloupes, thick, close netting on the rind indicates best quality. Cantaloupes are ripe when the stem scar is smooth and the space between the netting is yellow or yellow-green. They are best when fully ripe with fruity odor.

Honeydews are ripe when the rind has a creamy to yellowish color and velvety texture. Immature honeydews are whitish-green.

Ripe watermelons have some yellow color on one side. If melons are white or pale green on one side, they are not ripe.

Oranges, Grapefruit, and Lemons: Choose those heavy for their size. Smoother, thinner skins usually indicate more juice. Most skin markings do not affect quality. Oranges with a slight greenish tinge may be just as ripe as fully colored ones. Light or greenish-yellow lemons are more tart than deep yellow ones. Avoid citrus fruits showing withered, sunken or soft areas.

Measurements & Substitutions

Measurements

A pinch	1/8 tsp. or less
3 tbsp.	1 tablespoon
4 tbsp.	¼ cup
8 tbsp.	½ cup
12 tbsp.	¾ cup
16 tbsp.	1 cup
2 cups	1 pint
4 cups	1 quart
4 quarts	1 gallon
8 quarts	1 peck
4 pecks	1 bushel
16 ounces	1 pound
32 ounces	1 quart
1 ounce liquid	2 tbsp.
8 ounce liquid	1 cup

**Use standard measuring spoons and cups.
All measurements are level.**

Substitutions

Ingredient	Quantity	Substitute
Baking Powder	1 tsp.	¼ tsp. baking soda plus ½ tsp. cream of tarter
Ketchup or Chili Sauce	1 cup	1 cup tomato sauce plus ½ cup sugar and 2 tbsp. vinegar (for use in cooking)
Chocolate	1 square (1oz.)	3 or 4 tbsp. plus 1 tbsp. butter
Cornstarch	1 tbsp	2 tbsp. four or 2 tsp. quick tapioca
Cracker Crumbs	¾ cup	1 cup bread crumbs
Dates	1 lb.	1 ½ cup dates, pitted and cut
Dry Mustard	1 tsp.	1 tbsp. prepared mustard
Flour, Self-Rising	1 cup	1 cup all-purpose flour, ½ tsp. salt, and 1 tsp. baking powder
Herbs, Fresh	1 tbsp.	1 tsp. dried herbs
Milk, Sour	1 cup	1 tbsp. lemon juice or vinegar plus sweet milk to make 1 cup (let stand for 5 minutes)
Milk, Whole	1 cup	½ cup evaporated milk plus ½ cup water
Mini Marshmallows	10	1 large marshmallow
Onion, Fresh	1 small	1 tbsp. instant minced onion
Sugar, Brown	½ cup	2 tbsp. molasses in ½ cup granulated sugar
Sugar, Powdered	1 cup	1 cup granulated sugar plus 1 tsp. cornstarch
Tomato Juice	1 cup	½ cup tomato sauce plus ½ cup water

Equivalency Chart

Food	Quantity	Yield
Apple	1 medium	1 cup
Banana, mashed	1 medium	1/3 cup
Bread	1 ½ slices	1 cup soft crumbs
Bread	1 slice	¼ cup fine, dry crumbs
Butter	1 stick or ¼ lb.	½ cup
Cheese, American, cubed	1 lb.	2 2/3 cups
Cheese, American, grated	1 lb.	5 cups
Cheese, Cream Cheese	3 oz. package	6 2/3 tbsp
Chocolate, bitter	1 square	1 oz.
Cocoa	1 lb.	4 cups
Coconut	1 ½ lb. package	2 2/3 cups
Coffee, ground	1 lb.	5 cups
Cornmeal	1 lb.	3 cups
Cornstarch	1 lb.	3 cups
Crackers, Graham	14 squares	1 cup fine crumbs
Crackers, Saltine	28 squares	1 cup fine crumbs
Egg	4-5 whole	1 cup
Egg, Whites	8 – 10	1 cup
Egg, Yolks	10 – 12	1 cup
Evaporated Milk	1 cup	3 cups whipped
Flour, Cake, sifted	1 lb.	4 ½ cups
Flour, Rye	1 lb.	5 cups
Flour, White, sifted	1 lb.	4 cups
Flour, White un-sifted	1 lb.	3 ¾ cups
Gelatin, flavored	3 ¼ oz.	½ cup
Gelatin, unflavored	¼ oz.	1 tbsp.
Lemon	1 medium	3 tbsp. juice
Marshmallows	16	¼ lb.
Noodles, cooked	8 oz. package	7 cups
Noodles, uncooked	4 oz. (1 ½ cups)	2 – 3 cups cooked
Noodles, Macaroni, cooked	8 oz. cooked	6 cups
Noodles, Macaroni, uncooked	4 oz. (1 ¼ cups)	2 ¼ cups cooked
Noodles, Spaghetti, uncooked	7 oz.	4 cups cooked
Nuts, chopped	¼ lb.	1 cup
Nuts, Almonds	1 lb.	3 ½ cups

Nuts, Walnuts, broken	1 lb.	3 cups
Nuts, Walnuts, unshelled	1 lb.	1 ½ to 1 ¾ cups
Onion	1 medium	½ cup
Orange	3 – 4 medium	1 cup juice
Raisins	1 lb.	3 ½ cups
Rice, Brown	1 cup	4 cups cooked
Rice, Converted	1 cup	3 ½ cups cooked
Rice, Regular	1 cup	3 cups cooked
Rice, Wild	1 cup	4 cups cooked
Sugar, Brown	1 lb.	2 ½ cups
Sugar, Powdered	1 lb.	3 ½ cups
Sugar, White	1 lb.	2 cups
Vanilla Wafers	22	1 cup fine crumbs
Zwieback, crumbled	4	1 cup

Food Quantities
For Large Servings

	25 Servings	50 Servings	100 Servings

Beverages:

	25 Servings	50 Servings	100 Servings
Coffee	½ lb. and 1 ½ gallons water	1 lb. and 3 gallons water	2 lb. and 6 gallons water
Lemonade	10 – 15 lemons and 1 ½ gallons water	20 – 30 lemons and 3 gallons water	40 – 60 lemons and 6 gallons water
Tea	1/12 lb. and 1 ½ gallons water	1/6 lb. and 3 gallons water	1/3 lb. and 6 gallons water

Desserts:

	25 Servings	50 Servings	100 Servings
Layered Cake	1 12" cake	3 10" cakes	6 10" cakes
Sheet Cake	1 10" x 12" cake	1 12" x 20" cake	2 12" x 20" cakes
Watermelon	37 ½ lb.	75 lb.	150 lb.
Whipping Cream	¾ pint	1 ½ to 2 pints	3 – 4 pints

Ice Cream:

Brick	3 ¼ quarts	6 ½ quarts	13 quarts
Bulk	2 ¼ quarts	4 ½ quarts or 1 ¼ gallons	9 quarts or 2 ½ gallons

Meat, Poultry, or Fish:

Fish	13 lb.	25 lb.	50 lb.
Fish, fillets or steaks	7 ½ lb.	15 lb.	30 lb.
Hamburger	9 lb.	18 lb.	35 lb.
Turkey or Chicken	13 lb.	25 to 35 lb.	50 to 75 lb.
Wieners (beef)	6 ½ lb.	13 lb.	25 lb.

Salads or Casseroles:

Baked Beans	¾ gallon	1 ¼ gallons	2 ½ gallons
Jell-o Salad	¾ gallon	1 ¼ gallons	2 ½ gallons
Potato Salad	4 ¼ quarts	2 ¼ gallons	4 ½ gallons
Scalloped Potatoes	4 ½ quarts or 1 12" x 20" pan	9 quarts or 2 ¼ gallons	18 quarts or 4 ½ gallons
Spaghetti	1 ¼ gallons	2 ½ gallons	5 gallons

Sandwiches:

Bread	50 slices or 3 1 lb. loaves	100 slices or 6 1 lb. loaves	200 slices or 12 1 lb. loaves
Butter	½ lb.	1 lb.	2 lb.
Lettuce	1 ½ heads	3 heads	6 heads
Mayonnaise	1 cup	2 cups	4 cups

Mixed Filling:

Meat, Eggs, Fish	1 ½ quarts	3 quarts	6 quarts
Jam, Jelly	1 quart	2 quarts	4 quarts

Microwave Hints

1. Place an open box of hardened brown sugar in the microwave oven with 1 cup of water. Microwave on high for 1 ½ to 2 minutes for ½ lb. or 2 to 3 minutes for 1 lb.

2. Soften hard ice cream by microwaving it at 30% power. One pint will take 15 to 30 seconds; one quart, 30 to 45 seconds; and one-half gallon, 45 to 60 seconds.

3. To melt chocolate, place ½ lb. in glass bowl or measuring cup. Melt uncovered at 50% power for 3 – 4 minutes; stir after 2 minutes.

4. Soften one 8oz. package of cream cheese by microwaving at 30% power for 2 to 2 ½ minutes. One 3oz. package of cream cheese will soften in 1 ½ to 2 minutes.

5. A 4 ½ oz. carton of whipped topping will thaw in 1 minute on the defrost setting. Whipped topping should be slightly firm in the center, but it will blend well when stirred. Do not over thaw!

6. Soften jell-o that has set up too hard – perhaps you were to chill it until slightly thickened and forgot it. Heat on a low power setting for a very short time.

7. Heat hot packs. A wet fingertip towel will take about 25 seconds. It depends on the temperature of the water used to wet the towel.

8. To scald milk, cook 1 cup for 2 to 2 ½ minutes, stirring once each minute.

9. To make dry bread crumbs, cut 6 slices of bread into ½" cubes. Microwave in 3-quart casserole dish for 6 to 7 minutes, or until dry, stirring after 3 minutes. Crush in the blender.

10. Refresh stale potato chips, crackers, or other snacks of such type by putting a plateful in the microwave

for 30 – 45 seconds. Let stand for 1 minute to crisp. Cereals can also be crisped this way.

11. Nuts will be easier to shell if you place 2 cups of nuts in a 1-quart casserole dish with 1 cup water. Cook for 4 to 5 minutes and the nutmeats will slip out whole after cracking the shell.

12. Stamp collectors can place a few drops of water on a stamp to remove it from an envelope. Heat in the microwave for 20 seconds and the stamp will come off.

13. Using a round dish instead of a square one eliminates overcooked corners in baking cakes.

14. Sprinkle a layer of medium, finely chopped walnuts evenly onto the bottom and side of a ring pan or Bundt cake pan to enhance the looks and eating quality. Pour in batter and microwave as recipe directs.

15. Do not salt foods on the surface as it causes dehydration and toughens food. Salt after you remove from the oven unless the recipe calls for using salt in the mixture.

16. Heat left-over custard and use it as frosting for a cake.

17. Melt marshmallow cream. Half of a 7oz. jar will melt in 35 – 40 seconds on high. Stir to blend.

18. To toast coconut, spread ½ cup coconut in a pie plate and cook for 3 – 4 minutes, stirring every 30 seconds after 2 minutes. Watch closely, as it quickly browns.

19. To melt crystallized honey, heat uncovered jar on high for 30 – 45 seconds. If jar is large, repeat.

20. One stick of butter or margarine will soften in 1 minute when microwaved at 20% power.

Calorie Counter

Beverages:

Apple Juice, 6oz.	90
Coffee (black)	0
Cola Type, 12oz.	115
Cranberry Juice, 6oz.	115
Ginger Ale, 12oz.	115
Grape Juice, (from frozen concentrate), 6oz.	142
Lemonade, (from frozen concentrate), 6oz.	85
Milk, protein fortified, 1 cup	105
Milk, Skim, 1 cup	90
Milk, Whole, 1 cup	160
Orange Juice, 6oz.	85
Pineapple Juice, unsweetened, 6oz.	95
Root Beer	150
Tonic (quinine water) 12oz.	132

Breads:

Cornbread, 1 small square	130
Dumplings, 1 med.	70
French Toast, 1 slice	135
Melba Toast, 1 slice	25
Muffins, Blueberry, 1 muffin	110
Muffins, Bran, 1 muffin	106
Muffins, Corn, 1 muffin	125
Muffins, English, 1 muffin	280
Pancakes, 1 (4")	60
Pumpernickel, 1 slice	75
Rye, 1 slice	60
Waffle, 1	216
White, 1 slice	60 - 70
Whole Wheat, 1 slice	55 -

	65

Cereals:

Cornflakes, 1 cup	105
Cream of Wheat, 1 cup	120
Oatmeal, 1 cup	148
Rice Flakes, 1 cup	105
Shredded Wheat, 1 biscuit	100
Sugar Krisps, ¾ cup	110

Crackers:

Graham, 1 cracker	15 – 30
Rye Crisp, 1 cracker	35
Saltine, 1 cracker	17 – 20
Wheat Thins, 1 cracker	9

Dairy Products:

Butter or Margarine, 1 tbsp.	100
Cheese, American, 1oz.	100
Cheese, Camembert, 1oz.	85
Cheese, Cheddar, 1oz.	115
Cheese, Cottage Cheese, 1oz.	30
Cheese, Mozzarella, 1oz.	90
Cheese, Parmesan, 1oz.	130
Cheese, Ricotta, 1oz.	50
Cheese, Roquefort, 1 oz.	105
Cheese, Swiss, 1 oz.	105
Cream, light, 1 tbsp.	30
Cream, heavy, 1 tbsp.	55
Cream, sour, 1 tbsp.	45
Hot Chocolate, with Milk, 1 cup	277
Milk Chocolate, 1oz.	145 – 155
Yogurt made w/ whole milk, 1 cup	150 – 165
Yogurt made w/ skimmed milk, 1 cup	125

Eggs:

Fried, 1 large	100
Poached or Boiled, 1 large	75 – 80
Scrambled or in Omelet, 1 large	110 - 130

Fish and Seafood:

Bass, 4oz.	105
Salmon, broiled or baked, 3oz.	155
Sardines, canned in oil, 3oz.	170
Trout, fried, 3 ½ oz.	220
Tuna, in oil, 3oz.	170
Tuna, in water, 3oz.	110

Fruits:

Apple, 1 medium	80 – 100
Applesauce, sweetened, ½ cup	90 – 115
Applesauce, unsweetened, ½ cup	50
Banana, 1 medium	85
Blueberries, ½ cup	45
Cantaloupe, ½ cup	24
Cherries (pitted), raw, ½ cup	40
Grapefruit, ½ medium	55
Grapes, ½ cup	35 – 55
Honeydew, ½ cup	55
Mango, 1 medium	90
Orange, 1 medium	65 – 75
Peach, 1 medium	35
Pear, 1 medium	60 – 100
Pineapple, fresh, ½ cup	40
Pineapple, canned in syrup, ½ cup	95
Plum, 1 medium	30

Strawberries, fresh, ½ cup	30
Strawberries, frozen and sweetened, ½ cup	120 – 140
Tangerine, 1 large	39
Watermelon, ½ cup	42

Meat and Poultry:

Beef, Ground (lean), 3oz.	185
Beef, Roast, 3oz.	185
Chicken, broiled, 3oz.	115
Lamb Chop (lean), 3oz.	175 – 200
Steak, Sirloin, 3oz.	175
Steak, Tenderloin, 3oz.	174
Steak, Top Round, 3oz.	162
Turkey, dark meat, 3oz.	175
Turkey, white meat, 3oz.	150
Veal, Cutlet, 3oz.	156
Veal, Roast, 3oz.	76

Nuts:

Almonds, 2 tbsp.	105
Cashews, 2 tbsp.	100
Peanuts, 2 tbsp.	105
Peanut Butter, 1 tbsp.	95
Pecans, 2 tbsp.	95
Pistachios, 2 tbsp.	92
Walnuts, 2 tbsp.	80

Pasta:

Macaroni or Spaghetti, cooked, ¾ cup	115

Salad Dressings:

Blue Cheese, 1 tbsp.	70
French, 1 tbsp.	65
Italian, 1 tbsp.	80
Mayonnaise, 1 tbsp.	100
Olive Oil, 1 tbsp.	124

Russian, 1 tbsp.	70
Salad Oil, 1 tbsp.	120

Soups:

Bean, 1 cup	130 – 180
Beef Noodle, 1 cup	70
Bouillon and Consommé, 1 cup	30
Chicken Noodle, 1 cup	65
Chicken with Rice, 1 cup	50
Minestrone, 1 cup	80 – 150
Split Pea, 1 cup	145 – 170
Tomato with Milk	170
Vegetable	80 - 100

Vegetables:

Asparagus, 1 cup	35
Broccoli, cooked, ½ cup	25
Cabbage, cooked, ½ cup	15 – 20
Carrots, cooked, ½ cup	25 – 30
Cauliflower, ½ cup	10 – 15
Corn (kernels), ½ cup	70
Green Beans, 1 cup	30
Lettuce, shredded, ½ cup	5
Mushrooms, canned, ½ cup	20
Onions, cooked, ½ cup	30
Peas, cooked, ½ cup	60
Potato, baked, 1 medium	90
Potato, chips, 8 – 10	100
Potato, Mashed, w/ milk & butter, 1 cup	200 - 300
Spinach, 1 cup	40
Tomato, raw, 1 medium	25
Tomato, cooked, ½ cup	30

Cooking Terms

Au Gratin: Topped with crumbs and/or cheese and browned in oven or under broiler.

Au Jus: Served in its own juices.

Baste: To moisten foods during cooking with pan drippings or special sauce in order to add flavor and prevent drying.

Bisque: A thick cream soup.

Blanch: To immerse in rapidly boiling water and allowed to cook slightly.

Cream: To soften a fat, especially butter, by beating it at room temperature. Butter and sugar are often creamed together, making a smooth, soft paste.

Crimp: To seal the edges of a two-crust pie either by pinching them at intervals with the fingers or by pressing them together with the tongs of a fork.

Crudités: An assortment of raw vegetables (i.e. carrots, broccoli, celery, mushrooms) that is served as a hors d'oeuvre, often accompanied by a dip.

Degrease: To remove fat from the surface of stews, soups, or stock. It's usually cooled in the refrigerator so that fat hardens and is easily removed.

Dredge: To coat lightly with flour, cornmeal, etc.

Entrée: The main course.

Fold: To incorporate a delicate substance such as whipped cream or beaten egg whites, into another substance without releasing air bubbles. A spatula is used to gently bring part of the mixture from the bottom of the bowl to the top. The process is repeated, while slowly rotating the bowl, until the ingredients are thoroughly blended.

Glaze: To cover with a glossy coating, such as a melted and somewhat diluted jelly for fruit desserts.

Julienne: To cut vegetables, fruits, or cheeses into match-shaped silvers.

Marinate: To allow food to stand in a liquid in order to tenderize or to add flavor.

Meuniere: Dredged with flour and sautéed in butter.

Mince: To chop food into very small pieces.

Parboil: To boil until partially cooked; to blanch. Usually final cooking in a seasoned sauce follows this procedure.

Pare: To remove the outermost skin of a fruit or vegetable.

Poach: To cook gently in hot liquid kept just below the boiling point.

Puree: To mash foods by hand by rubbing through a sieve or food mill, or by whirling in a blender or food processor until perfectly smooth.

Refresh: To run cold water over food that has been parboiled in order to stop the cooking process quickly.

Sauté: To cook and/or brown food in a small quantity of hot shortening.

Scald: To heat to just below the boiling point, when tiny bubbles appear at the edge of the saucepan.

Simmer: To cook in liquid just below the boiling point. The surface of the liquid should be barely moving, broken from time to time by slowly rising bubbles.

Steep: to let food stand in hot liquid in order to extract or to enhance flavor, like tea in hot water or poached fruit in sugar syrup.

Toss: To combine ingredients with a repeated lifting motion.

Whip: To beat rapidly in order to incorporate air and produce expansion, as in heavy cream or egg whites.